BEVERLY CARRADINE

I0180583

The Second Blessing In Symbol

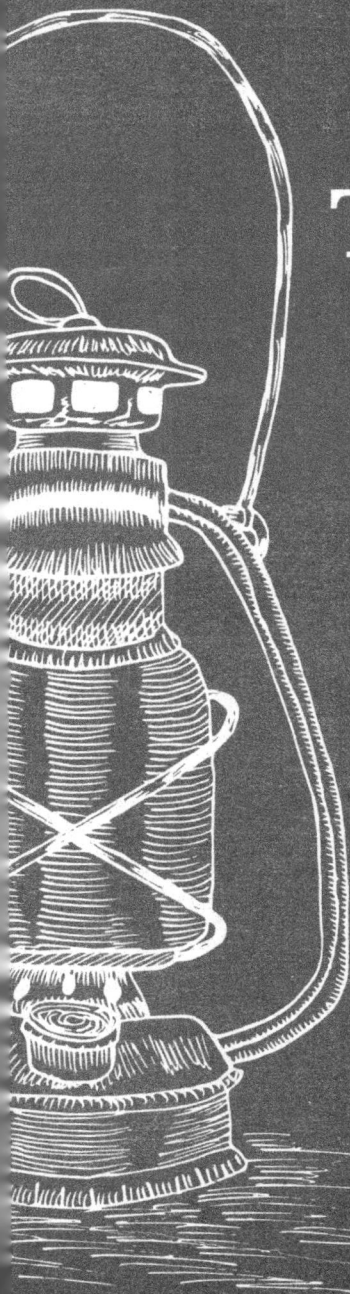

First Fruits

THE ACADEMIC OPEN PRESS OF ASBURY SEMINARY

The Second Blessing in Symbol

by

Beverly Carradine

First Fruits Press
Wilmore, Kentucky
c2015

The Second Blessing in Symbol, by Beverly Carradine

First Fruits Press, © 2015
Previously published by the L.L. Pickett, 1894, 1893.

ISBN: 9781621714439 (print), 9781621714446 (digital), 9781621714453 (kindle)

Digital version at http://place.asburyseminary.edu/firstfruitsheritagematerial/117/

First Fruits Press is a digital imprint of the Asbury Theological Seminary, B.L. Fisher Library. Asbury Theological Seminary is the legal owner of the material previously published by the Pentecostal Publishing Co. and reserves the right to release new editions of this material as well as new material produced by Asbury Theological Seminary. Its publications are available for noncommercial and educational uses, such as research, teaching and private study. First Fruits Press has licensed the digital version of this work under the Creative Commons Attribution Noncommercial 3.0 United States License. To view a copy of this license, visit http://creativecommons.org/licenses/by-nc/3.0/us/.

For all other uses, contact:

First Fruits Press
B.L. Fisher Library
Asbury Theological Seminary
204 N. Lexington Ave.
Wilmore, KY 40390
http://place.asburyseminary.edu/firstfruits

Cover design by Kelli Dierdorf

asburyseminary.edu
800.2ASBURY
204 North Lexington Avenue
Wilmore, Kentucky 40390

First Fruits
THE ACADEMIC OPEN PRESS OF ASBURY SEMINARY

First Fruits Press
The Academic Open Press of Asbury Theological Seminary
204 N. Lexington Ave., Wilmore, KY 40390
859-858-2236
first.fruits@asburyseminary.edu
asbury.to/firstfruits

REV. B. CARRADINE, D D.

THE SECOND BLESSING

IN SYMBOL.

———

BY REV. B. CARRADINE, D.D.,
Author of "Sanctification," "A Journey to Palestine," etc.

SECOND EDITION, ENLARGED.
PRICE $1.

L. L. PICKETT,
PUBLISHER OF "HOLINESS," AND OTHER RELIGIOUS LITERATURE,
COLUMBIA, S. C.
1894.

3

4

PREFACE.

THE author of this book, although a young man, wields one of the most familiar and welcome pens to our Methodism, hence needs no introduction.

The types and symbols of the Old Testament evidently contain as deep a spiritual meaning as the parables of the New Testament, and the whole combine in the revelation of the great doctrines of Christianity. The perfect harmony existing between these two books unites them into one Book. The great doctrine of the Book, the doctrine toward which all other doctrines lead, and in which they all center, is the doctrine of holiness. That God wills, provides for, and demands our entire sanctification from all sin, no candid Bible reader will deny. Methodism teaches in her standards of doctrine that entire sanctification is wrought in the believer's heart subsequent to justification; her founders preached, and her charter members professed, sanctification as a second work of grace. Those who will take the pains to seek will find it so recorded in the sermons, songs, and history of the early Methodists.

Our author undertakes to show in this book that this doctrine, the second work of grace, is taught in the types and symbols of the Bible.

Our prayer is that those who read this book may have the faith that will make them able "to enter into the holiest by the blood of Jesus, by a new and living way, which he hath consecrated for us."   H. C. MORRISON, *Evangelist.*

(5)

CONTENTS.

(6)

8 *Contents.*

THE SECOND BLESSING IN SYMBOL.

CHAPTER I.

A FEW OPENING WORDS.

THE question that is agitating the Church to-day is whether there is a second and distinct work of God in the soul following that of regeneration. It appears in papers, pulpits, camp meetings, Conference love feasts, and elsewhere. Wherever and whenever it is sprung there is seen agitation. It is beyond doubt the real question before the Church to-day. There is none that can compare to it. If God has a second work or blessing for the soul, out of which Satan has cheated the Church, ought not men to know it? If, as the advocates of holiness say, this blessing touches the wealth and activities of the Church and transforms the membership into glowing, burning messengers of Christ, is it not an important, vital, all-essential question?

With many on the opposing side the conviction is honest that the advocates of a second divine work are mistaken and deluded. Forgetful of the fact that the Bible calls it "the secret of the Lord," they expect to know all about it without using the means by which alone the secret can be obtained. It is a conditional blessing, and yet they look to understand what cannot be known except through the compliance with these conditions. Experience alone can bring understanding of sanctification as it does of regeneration. A person cannot know a road until he has gone along its length, and yet here are people who have not trod this way of holiness, nor made the effort that will alone place them in it, doubting and denying the fact that there is such a way.

Many make merry over the term "second blessing," although it is both Wesleyan and scriptural. Such merriment only pains the heart of the advocate of holiness, as a laugh about conversion stabs the spirit of the regenerated man. In both cases the feeling is that the laugh or jest is ill-timed, misdirected, and ignorantly aimed at the work of the Holy One. In either case "they know not what they do." But the merriment is to be met as Christ received the gibes around the cross. If the blessing is true and scriptural and divine, it will sustain us, while it will also endure and survive every kind of rough treatment. If it is of man, it will come to naught; but if it is of

God it will certainly triumph; but alas! for them who should be found fighting against God.

The charge made upon us in high quarters is that we are deluded. This is certainly a grave and sweeping charge. It takes in a great many people. It arraigns hundreds of thousands through the land. The charge also takes in people of great celebrity: such a man as Fenelon, and such a woman as Madam Guyon; such men as Asbury, McKendree, Fletcher, Benson, Clarke, of early days, and such women as Phœbe Palmer, Frances Havergal, Frances Willard, and Hannah Whitehall Smith, of later times.

The thoughtful mind is hardly prepared to believe that such people, and so many people, living at wide intervals of time and distance from each other, and without possibility of or motive for collusion, could be possessed by so marvelous and general a delusion. Reason and common sense rebel against such a supposition. Now when in addition to this the experience of these people is found to coincide exactly with a teaching that runs through the Bible how is it possible for one to pronounce the whole matter a delusion?

Who wonders that a Church which doubts and disputes through its journals, pulpits, and chief officers the fact of such a grace and blessing should fail to see it? It is the eye of faith, not doubt, that discerns what Paul calls the " second grace," and John Wesley termed the " second blessing." Who wonders that men, gifted, learned, religious, and useful, should fail to enter into the holy of holies when they have neglected the laver at the door, and the SECOND application of blood which Moses and Paul agree in saying was necessary as the condition of entrance? Who wonders that any man should fail in this holy experience if he realizes a reservation somewhere in the life, knows there is a room in the heart where Christ is not allowed to enter, a closet where something is withheld or concealed, or is conscious of a wrong unrighted or a confession unmade? What if there be such things as pride, bitterness, ecclesiastical revenge, ambition for place, lust for oratorical honors, and the praise of men, and things even lower? What if a man's heart should become influenced with the desire for the office of a bishop, and should speak, write, and attitudinize to that end? What if a man indulges in habits unclean and expensive, and exhorts the poor of his congregation to contribute their hard earnings to the support of the ministry and the gospel, and then proceeds in the full sight of the congregation and heaven to puff into smoke or expectorate in tobacco much of that self-denial and consecrated money upon the ground?

Does the reader think that a partially consecrated man can know the MYSTERY of the gospel, take in the tender secret of the Lord, and be familiar with what is beyond the veil, although that veil be rent from top to bottom? The fact that it is rent does not disclose or expose the most holy place. A curtain rent from top to bottom is not pulled down; but the torn edges hang side by side together, and the things beyond are still concealed. Christ has not made holiness common to all, but possible to all. The veil is rent, but the veil is still there.

Now, will the Holy Ghost reveal the holiest to a partially consecrated man? Would God let a priest enter the holy of holies with an unclean habit? Will he do it now? The man may be gifted, learned, admirable for many reasons, a power in certain lines, and honored by his Church with elevated positions and offices, and yet these things in themselves will not suffice to bring one within the veil, into the secret place of the Most High.

Would the reader lay bare the tender secrets of his soul to one who was not in perfect sympathy and accord with him? Would God do so? Who marvels that some men, looking toward the most holy place of the tabernacle, declare that they see nothing—that there is nothing? This, however, does not prove that there is nothing, but simply that these men see nothing.

A certain well-known man said a long time ago that we must " cleanse ourselves from ALL filthiness of the flesh and spirit " if we would perfect holiness. He who will not do this will never know what Paul meant by " perfecting holiness." It will always seem to him a vague, indistinct, never to be attained blessedness. But to the man who obeys the word and fulfills the condition, the experience itself, beautiful, blessed, and abiding, will come. The heart's vision of God, the rest of faith, the joy of purity, the sweetness of perfect love, the upwellings of constant praise, and the thrill of constant victory through Christ will become the soul's portion and heritage forever.

CHAPTER II.

THE word " second " seems to be especially disagreeable and offensive to many, and grave objections are urged against the expression.

We would say that we are no stickler for terms, and think it best in describing a divine work of grace to adhere to scriptural phraseology. But when a term like that of the " second blessing " does no violence to the Word of God, but is really descriptive of a work that we find taught in the Bible, then it seems it might be used without offense or objection. For instance, Christ promises his disciples another blessing. He commanded them not to leave Jerusalem until they obtained it. He called it the " promise of the Father," a " baptism," " enduement of power," and the " Holy Ghost coming down upon them." All of these terms plainly indicate something new to be received and experienced by the disciples. The "promise of the Father" was something yet unfulfilled, they had not yet been " endued with power," and according to the Saviour's words the Holy Ghost had not yet come upon them. He had breathed the Spirit upon them, but there was something yet evidently to be realized. As for the word " baptism," it cannot be tortured in any way tò mean " birth;" for these two things are always distinct, and separated by an interval of time, both in nature and grace. Moreover, when this baptism—enduement—promise of the Father came upon the disciples on the day of Pentecost it was seen to be another work of the Spirit, different from anything they had experienced before in the spiritual life. If this statement is challenged, we bring up in proof the apostle Peter, who declares in Acts xv. 8, 9 that it was a purifying of their hearts by faith. He identifies here the blessing received by Cornelius with what came upon them at Pentecost. This verse is a fatal blow to Zinzendorfianism, and to those of our Church who insist that regeneration is purity; and it is one of the many foundation stones we have upon which to rest the doctrine of the second blessing.

So here is a subsequent work of grace, and as such can be truly called a second blessing. Furthermore, as both in the Bible and in the Christian experience " a baptism of the spirit " is recognized to be different from " the baptism of the Holy Spirit," this latter-named experience can truly be called the second blessing. Right here we should cease enumerating: first, for the reason that after sanctification a child of God should receive so many blessings that he cannot count them; and secondly, because there are but two complete works of grace wrought in the soul by the Spirit. And just as any number of manifestations of God to the world fails to increase the number of persons in the Godhead, so numerous blessings, no matter how frequent and rich, cannot be scripturally distinguished by the terms third, fourth, fifth, and so on *ad infinitum.* There is but one work of grace, purifying and transforming, that is subsequent to regeneration. With this additional blessing man enters into heaven. After this there is nothing left on earth or in heaven but constant and everlasting growth in grace. Hence the humorous and unkind fling by some at those who hold the second blessing, saying that they have gone much farther along in the spiritual numerals; that they have received the one hundredth blessing, etc. This fling loses all of its force from the lack of knowledge it shows of the two distinct works of the Holy Spirit. We repeat here that there are thousands of " a baptisms " in the Christian life, but there is but one " the baptism." There are hundreds of blessings that break upon and fill the

2

believing heart, but there is but one second blessing.   Let every Methodist preacher who reads
these lines answer what was it that he in his ordination vows at Conference promised God and the
Methodist Church to " groan " to obtain.   A vow
made up of scriptural terms.   Certainly it was not
a covenant, oath, or pledge to " grow."   Every
sensible man knows that both in nature and grace
growth takes place quietly as the result of healthy
conditions, and there is no need of agonizing,
straining, or groaning to accomplish or accelerate
what is secured by the quiet workings of a noise-
less law.   The very language of the Discipline
where we are pledged to " groan after " something
that we have not declares that it is an obtainment of
grace which cannot be secured on lines of growth;
and hence is our Church's confirmation of the fact
that there is a second blessing.

Besides all this we advance the thought that the
term " second blessing " is more scriptural than
some imagine.   If King James's translators had
been truer to the original in 2 Corinthians i. 15,
we would have to-day the words " second grace "
instead of " second benefit."   The Greek word
translated " benefit " is *charis*.   If any Greek
scholar should be asked what this word meant in
the original, he never would reply " benefit," but

"grace," "divine grace," "divine gift," etc. The word *charis* is found over one hundred and fifty times in the New Testament, and in every instance is translated " grace " except at this place. Here the prominent definition of the word is avoided and a weaker meaning taken up by the translators.

Paul alludes to this second grace in Romans v. 2: " By whom *also* we have access by faith *into this grace.*" Here is an additional grace, and entered upon through another act of faith in Christ. James speaks of it in the words: " He giveth more [another] grace." Excellent Greek scholars say that the word in brackets is the proper word of the text. In Hebrews ix. 28 the second work appears again in the words: " Unto them that *look for him* shall he appear the second time without sin unto salvation." We know this is claimed to describe the fact of Christ's return to the earth in judgment, but we call the reader's attention to two statements in the verse that destroy that claim. One is that this coming is " unto salvation," whereas the last day brings judgment; Christ will come then as a Judge. Again we know at the judgment day " every eye shall see him," but the verse quoted declares something different in the words, " Unto them that *look for him* shall He appear the second time." Some regenerated people are not looking for him. The condition of receiving Christ in full salvation or holiness is "looking." The disciples "looked" for ten days, and were not disappointed in Christ's coming. They got that day what they had never obtained before. Their lives proved afterward that they had received the second blessing.

We quote Paul again in Galatians iv. 19: "My little children, of whom I travail in birth *again* until Christ be formed in you." Let the reader emphasize the word " again " as we have done. Let him attend a holiness altar service, and he will see two things not soon forgotten—*viz.*, a second travail of spirit among Christians, and " Christ formed " in regenerated people in distinctness and power as never before.

But the question may be asked: "Why did the translators in King James's time use the weaker meaning ' benefit ' instead of the stronger, truer definition ' grace?' " The answer comes readily: That, like some people to-day, they were ignorant of this tender, holy, heart experience. The blessing of Pentecost, or sanctification by faith, was unknown to them, just as justification by faith was to many in Luther's time. If one doctrine can be lost for awhile, why not another? These men did not know what Paul was talking about when he

said in the original text: " I was minded to come
unto you before, that ye might have a second
grace." Perhaps they thought he meant his trip
or visit, or some collection of eastern curiosities.
But the word *charis* would not allow such a diver-
gence from its real meaning, and so they put down
the word " benefit " in the text, and wrote the true
definition, " grace," in the margin, where it can be
found to-day. Let the reader turn to his Bible and
see for himself.

When we remember that these same men, in 1
Corinthians xiii. 5, translated as follows, " Charity
is not easily provoked," when one of the best Greek
scholars in the land says that the original text will
not justify the presence of the word " easily," but
reads, " Charity is not provoked," and when we
bear in mind that love is *not* provoked, but that
anger or the sense of justice is provoked; when
we remember this we begin to get light upon
those famous scholars whom it has been so fashionable to praise. King James was a choleric
man according to history. In deference to his oc-
casional fits of passion these men accommodated
the Word of God to their royal reader (even as is
done to-day in many Churches), and wrote that
charity was not easily provoked. Let the reader
open his Bible and read the first paragraph of the

prefatory address of these translators to King
James, and see their fulsome praise or flattery of
a carnal man, and say whether they were best able
to understand the holy mysteries of the gospel oftentimes hidden in the shaded meaning of a word.
Paul speaks of a " hidden life." Alas that it is
hidden to so many to-day!

To return to the verse first quoted in regard to
the second grace. Paul had on his first visit to
Corinth brought pardon and salvation to the people through the blood of Christ. They heard, believed, were saved, and a Church was founded.
Paul departs, and from afar writes to them that he
was minded to come again that they might have a
second grace. What grace? Not simply an hour's
emotion arising from the preaching of a sermon;
not a fresh experience of grace as we all ought to
have each day; not a new fruit of the Spirit, because in regeneration we get all the fruits of the
Spirit. Paul certainly would not desire to cross
lands and seas just to get a few people happy for
an hour or so. He meant what Christ referred to
when he told the disciples to tarry at Jerusalem for
another work of grace and blessing that was to
come upon them. Paul meant a grace which he
had not at first presented in his stay at Corinth,
even as Christ had kept it back for three years in

Judea, then letting it descend on the day of Pentecost.

He meant what the makers of our Discipline had in mind when they inserted in the ordination service a solemn vow or oath for every preacher to take. In this vow he declares to the bishop that he expects to be " *made* perfect in love in this life," not grow perfect. He also declares that he is " *groaning* after it," not growing. When he obtains what he vows he is groaning after it is the second blessing. We never knew one who had really obtained what the Discipline thus requires but was perfectly willing to call it the second blessing.

Yes, there is a " second grace." John the Baptist called it " the baptism of the Holy Ghost and fire." Christ called it " the promise of the Father," " enduement of power," and in John, seventeenth chapter, alludes to it in the word " sanctify." Paul named it " his rest," " perfection," " more excellent way," " second grace," " sanctification," and " holiness." John writes it " perfect love." These are not all of the scriptural terms used to describe this blessing, but only a few gathered hastily, each one, however, bearing on its face the fact that it represents something higher than regeneration.

Madam Guyon called it the " rest of faith," and was put in prison for declaring the doctrine and living the experience.   It took her years to bring Cardinal Fénelon into the blessing, but at last he saw and obtained it, and wrote powerfully on the subject.   Dr. Upham terms it " the interior life." John Wesley gave it the title that is so objectionable to some of our brethren—viz., " the second blessing "—and Charles Wesley in his beautiful numbers describes it as the " second rest."   We conclude this chapter with a stanza from Hymn 444 in our Church hymn book:

> Breathe, O breathe thy loving Spirit
>   Into every troubled breast!
> Let us all in thee *inherit*,
>   Let us *find* that *second rest:*
> Take away our bent to sinning;
>   Alpha and Omega be;
> End of faith, as its beginning,
>   Set our hearts at liberty.

If there be no second blessing, the Methodist Church is seriously at fault in allowing such expressions as those above to appear in her hymn book.   Furthermore, she stands to-day convicted of the strangest inconsistency and contradictoriness when, after making her preachers " groan " to obtain a second blessing of " perfect love," she immediately proceeds to make them " groan " again because they HAVE obtained it.

CHAPTER III.

THE Bible throughout recognizes and teaches a double work in salvation. Toplady voices this in his hymn now sung by the Christian world:

Be of sin the double cure.

So there is a twofold cure in redemption: one the regenerating and the other the sanctifying grace of God; the first bringing pardon and peace, and the second purity and power.

If this is a fact, we may expect to see the proof all through the Scriptures, and different kinds of proof at that. The author in his study of the word has discovered no less than six distinct lines of proof therein establishing the fact of the double cure in salvation. Five of these scriptural methods of proof appear in his book entitled " Holiness and Its Witnesses," while the sixth is made to appear in this volume. The argument in this book for the second blessing is based altogether on the proof found in symbolism. Just as Christ was typified in the lamb, altar, and high priest; regeneration, in the washing of the laver; the resurrection, in the waving of the first sheaf of the

(25)

harvest; so holiness, or the second blessing, the great work of Christ in the soul, is symbolized in an equally impressive manner and indeed far more frequently.

This book does not pretend to treat the subject exhaustively. The many calls and duties of a city pastorate have prevented that finish and completeness desired by the writer, while other reasons have diminished the size of this volume, that could have very easily and delightfully to the author been much larger in its contents.

It constitutes one of the charms of Bible study to discover in the forms, ceremonies, washings, anointings, and in the very drapery and sacred furniture of the tabernacle, the deep truths of the kingdom of Christ that have been thus imbedded and hidden away for the recognition and future use of all generations.

It is wonderful how the two blessings thus appear in the Word of God. The very division of the Bible into two Testaments and covenants contains thought for the reflective mind; one the Bible says brought perfection, the other did not. And the cloven tongues of fire at Pentecost have back of them voices of testimony. Why were they cloven? Surely no one will think this peculiar sight to be without design. The fire symbolizes the presence and work of the Holy Ghost, and the cleaving or dividing of the flame on each head into two parts declares the two works of grace.

There seems to be more than one purpose in this object lesson method of teaching spiritual truths. One advantage is that Satan is foiled in his endeavor to penetrate the word, work, and purposes of God. If the angels themselves bend over the mysteries of grace in a vain effort to comprehend them, how much more will fallen spirits fail to understand the deep things of God? If the devil had been able to read symbols before their fulfillment, he would never have crucified Christ. The wisdom of veiling truths and coming victories in imagery is seen in the book of Revelation; for if those inspired chapters could have been understood eighteen hundred years ago, what an advantage would have been possessed by Satan and evil men.

Again, the veiling of certain truths in typical form secures that freedom of spirit which man must have to fully accomplish the design and desire of God.

Still again, the very veiling inflames the soul with ardor for the pursuit and possession of that which is just before it half revealed and half concealed. Besides this, the fact of certain truths buried here and there in the Word of God arouses the spirit of reading and study, causes faith to be strengthened with each additional discovery, and makes the Bible the most fascinating of books.

Of course there is a danger of running symbolism farther than God intended, and this should be avoided. But this is not any more to be deplored than to see in the Scripture the wonderful temple, the impressive service, the rich and beautiful drapery and furniture, the washings, wavings, sprinklings, anointings, and burnings, and suppose they mean nothing. What thoughtful mind can believe these things were to gratify the eye? Whose spiritual heart could suppose that they were appointed to foster and satisfy Church pride? Who so stupid as to think they meant nothing?

While all of us will admit that the entire Levitical ritual elevated the minds of the people from low, groveling views of God; yet a humble, patient, prayerful study of that ritual, with the other types, will reveal that the whole history and work of grace, and especially the doctrine and experience of holiness, can be found in the symbols of the Bible.

CHAPTER IV.

The Manna in the Holy Place.

EVERY reader knows that the manna typified Christ and his salvation. It was gathered and eaten by the people; was sweet to the taste; preserved life; had to be gathered every morning; and melted away as the day advanced.

If this is not a true picture of the regenerated life, then have we failed to see, hear, and feel correctly. We eat of the true bread that comes down from heaven; it is sweet to the soul; it has to be struggled for each morning; it seems to melt and disappear as the day advances. The close of the day, even its noon, finds many Christians feeling they have none left. We have known some whose religion seemed to be gone by ten o'clock.

Now see a higher blessing taught through this same manna. It was taken and placed in the holy of holies, and there in the ark it remained for any number of days, for any sweep of years, pure, sweet, incorruptible, and unchangeable.

In this most impressive way God teaches us that our personal salvation is brought "within the veil," brought into the secret place of God's perpetual presence; in a word, into the state, life, and experience of holiness, and that then our religious life will be marked by an abiding sweetness and purity, by incorruptibleness and enduring power. It does not then require tremendous efforts to gather and retain the grace of God. The grace itself does not melt away at nine o'clock nor is it gone at twelve nor in the afternoon nor at night. It abides, and it abides sweet and pure, through the preserving power of the second blessing, which is the sanctifying grace of God. There is a religious experience which wastes away in the camp, grows hungry, and has to be periodically restored. There is another where the divine food and life is lodged within the heart, and the man with this inward, abiding nourishment knows no emptiness, wastings, or exhaustions, but is constantly filled. Meet him at any time, early in the day or late, in cloudy days or bright, in religious meetings or on the street, on Monday or on Sunday, he is always full. The manna is within, and it abides. John alludes to this second grace in Revelation ii. 17, where he says: " To him that overcometh will I give to eat of the *hidden* manna." The manna in the camp stood for salvation, but brought within the holy place it teaches a second and deeper experience which is called full salvation or holiness.

The Two Animals.

The very fact that two animals were required by the Levitical law to be presented for the sin offering is enough to arouse thought. This alone shows what is plainly taught elsewhere in the Bible, and taught as well in the Discipline and hymn book and standards of our Church, that there are two kinds of sin: personal and inherited, individual guilt and inborn depravity.

The offering up of one animal would not bring out this doubleness of the nature of iniquity; hence the law said bring two animals. In one place it is two goats. In another place the blood of a bullock and the blood of a goat are shed for the sin offering. Think of these two animals—the bullock and goat—and see how God brings out the natures of sin.

The goat nature is a more radical and offensive type than that of the bullock. Carnality is different from, deeper, harder to deal with, older and more venomous than one's personal or individual sinful nature and life.

A still more remarkable fact appears in what was

done to the two goats, which brings out still more clearly the two works of grace. One goat was slain. The second was led away into the wilderness bearing the iniquity of the people.

In regeneration we know not what becomes of our personal sins; they fairly melt away in the presence of Christ. In sanctification there is an unmistakable consciousness that the iniquity of the heart is TAKEN AWAY.

So we see that it requires the blood of two animals of different species, the bullock and goat, and besides this two animals of like species, two goats, but dealt with differently in order to teach the double nature of sin and the double work of Christ in the soul.

> Be of sin the DOUBLE cure,
> Save from wrath and make me pure.

The Two Birds.

Leprosy is the acknowledged type of sin. In the cleansing of the leper two birds were used. And two because sin is twofold or double. One bird was killed; the other bird was let " loose into the open field."

Here is a twofold treatment of sin: expiation and deliverance. Something is atoned for, and something is taken away. It harmonizes with the preceding symbol. The scapegoat disappears in the wilderness; the bird vanishes in the open air.

It harmonizes with the experience. The first work of grace atones for our sins and brings pardon; the second grace or blessing removes the principle of iniquity, the body of sin, and takes it away we know not where.

The Levites and Priests.

It has been customary to regard these two orders of Israel as foreshadowing two ranks and grades in the ministry. But we fail to hear a syllable fall from the lips of Christ, the great Head of the Church, in regard to elders and deacons or, indeed, any other named order of ministers. The whole body of preachers in his day were covered by the general term " disciples," and he was careful to say that if any of them should be greatest let him become the servant of the rest.

This fact alone is sufficient to arouse the thought that the priests and Levites stand for two grades in the spiritual life. Another fact that confirms this supposition is the statement of John that Christ has " made us kings and priests unto God." This was no allusion to the ministry, but was uttered in reference simply to the followers of Christ who

3

had realized a distinguishing grace at his hands. The word " us " takes in preacher and layman.

The difference between the priests and Levites was marked. There was a difference of dress, of table fare, and of approach to and waiting upon the tabernacle or temple. The priest went where the Levite did not and could not go.

There are priests and Levites in the spiritual life to-day. There are followers of Christ who are clothed in the white linen of purity that others do not wear. They eat of heavenly fare that their brethren neither have nor believe in. They come boldly " into the holiest," that is hidden by a veil from the eyes of other followers of God. And they offer sacrifices, minister, and labor about the altar, and conduct sacred services of all kinds in the home, social circle, class meeting, prayer meeting, and house of God, and do it easily, joyfully, and unctuously, in the presence of other servants of the Lord who stand by with dumb tongues, sinking hearts, and hands powerless or slow to lay hold upon the work of God. An additional suggestive fact is seen in the Levite paying tithes to the priest. The writer well recalls the homage he rendered a sanctified soul in the days before he received the blessing of holiness. The consciousness is in the regenerated man that his sanctified brother has a type of purity superior to his own. The Levite still pays tithes to the priest.

One other thing worthy of mention is that upon the brow of the priest shone the golden plate, bearing on it the words: "Holiness unto the Lord." The Levite did not have this, although he was a servant of God. Who is surprised that Christ came to "purify the sons of Levi" and make us all "priests unto God?" It is better to be a priest than a Levite: better because it brings us into a higher religious experience than we had before; better because it gives easier and greater access to God; and better because it plants in the heart and writes on the face "Holiness unto the Lord."

May the reader never rest until he has been taken from the courts of the temple and put in the holy place—in a word, changed from a Levite to a priest!

CHAPTER V.

The Two Washings of the Leper.

LET the reader turn to the fourteenth chapter of Leviticus, verses 8 and 9, and he will be struck with the fact that two washings of the body of the leper were required before God pronounced him clean.

Remember that leprosy is the pronounced type of sin in the Bible. The leper is the sinner. In the eighth verse he is said to wash himself and garments that he might be clean. It is remarkable that while immediately afterward he is allowed to come into the camp, yet God does not say that he is clean. In the ninth verse it is stated that *after seven days* the man underwent a *second* washing both of body and clothing. In this verse the following facts appear: First, that there was a second washing or cleansing; next, that there was a distinct interval of time between the two purifications; third, that God did not pronounce the leper

(36)

clean until after the second cleansing. It was then, and not till then, that the Scripture says: " He shall be clean."

He who can read this passage and fail to be impressed with the significance of the facts stated in it, and that so clearly bring out the two works of grace is little likely to be moved and convinced by anything that he finds in the Word of God.

The Two Washings of the Leprous Garment.

This appears in Leviticus xiii. 58. Let it be remembered that leprosy is the type of sin in the Bible. The garment or robe represents the soul. In Revelation the redeemed are said to have " washed their robes, and made them white in the blood of the lamb." Evidently the human spirit is referred to here. The leprous garment stands then for the sin-stained soul.

This garment had a first washing. It doubtless looked clean, and many no doubt pronounced it so. The first cleansing of the soul by the washing of regeneration has been thought by many to be a perfect purification. But God does not say so. Neither will Christians who have had but one cleansing testify in public that they have pure hearts. This is significant.

At the command of God the leprous garment

received a second washing, and then, and not till then, was it pronounced clean. Hear the words of God: " It shall be washed the *second* time, and shall be clean." How all this must strike a thoughtful person! Certainly it is a most vivid and impressive way of teaching the second work of grace in the soul, followed immediately by the voice of God witnessing its purity.

The Two Anointings of the Leper.

The first was with the blood of a lamb. This blood was placed on the right ear, thumb of the right hand, and great toe of the right foot.

The second anointing was with oil. It was placed like the blood upon the ear, thumb, and toe, but in addition to this was poured upon the head.

There was a distinct interval of time between the two transactions in order to punctuate clearly the two great works of God.

It was after the anointing of oil, and not till then, that the leper was declared to be clean.

Every item in this narration is significant. The blood always stands for Christ; the oil always for the Holy Ghost. In regeneration the man's body with its members are given to the service of Christ; the ear, hand, and foot have entered into a new service and are touched with the sign of their new Master and Lord.

In sanctification the oil of holiness is poured upon these same members, and a higher work is thus plainly taught. It was not until the holy oil was placed upon the vessels of the tabernacle that they were called holy. But not only does the oil itself call attention to a different work of grace; but the fact that it was poured upon the head! The anointing of the head emphasizes the fact of something additional and something higher in the spiritual life subsequent to regeneration.

"Thou anointest my head with oil; my cup runneth over." It always does. It did with the blood-washed disciples when God poured the oil of sanctification upon them on the day of Pentecost. The anointed head was there. The tongue of lambent flame over each brow declared what had come down upon them. And as a consequence their cups ran over. Let him that doubts their joy read the second chapter of Acts. When the oil is placed upon the blood, and the head and heart anointing takes place, the cup of joy is bound to run over.

The Scripture says that it was AFTER THE ANOINTING OF OIL that the leper was CLEAN.

So it is with the heart once leprous with sin. It

is the first work of God to pardon; the second work is to make holy.   And when the Holy Ghost descends a second time upon the waiting, believing soul that work is done.   The soul cries out in rapture, "I am pure!" the Spirit witnesses, "Thou art sanctified;" and the Book says, "He is clean."   "I am"—"thou art"—"he is." This is a part of the spiritual grammar that thrills the soul.   What reader of these lines can decline sanctification after this manner?

CHAPTER VI.

EVERY Bible reader knows that the tabernacle was divided into two rooms or sanctuaries. These two rooms were variously called the first and second, the outer and inner, the holy place and most holy place, or the holy of holies. But while the reader remembers the fact of the two apartments, very few have stopped to ask why there were two and what they represented. Some have a vague idea that the inner room referred to heaven, but the greater number of people sink down helplessly before the tabernacle, regarding the whole thing as an unsolvable mystery, when, if prayerfully studied, the rooms and furniture furnish great light for the proper understanding of the spiritual life, and with a powerful symbolic teaching clear up mysteries and reveal the way of holiness.

As is well known, the altar with its sacrifice before the tabernacle stood for Christ's suffering and death, and so represented our justification. The laver with its pure water, standing between

(41)

the altar and the tabernacle, symbolized regeneration.

The first room, or outer sanctuary, stood for the regenerated life. On entering was to be observed the seven-pronged candlestick, or lamp, on the right. There is beautiful light in the converted life. On the left side was a table with twelve loaves of bread. So there is nourishment, and strength as well. Immediately in front was a table from which incense arose twice or thrice a day. This last typified the prayers that go up regularly to God from the soul redeemed from the world and translated into his kingdom. This room was called the holy place, and here Paul tells us the priests accomplished the service of God. According to this the regenerated life is a holy life, and those living in it can and do please God.

There remained, however, these facts that suggested something better in the Christian life: One was that the candle or lamp had to be frequently replenished and carefully watched, or the light would go out. Indeed, in one place it is said that the " lamp of God burned low." Truly the regenerated man understands all about this. He feels often that he would love to help others to shine if he did not have such difficulty in keeping his own lamp bright. Then, while there was bread upon the table, it became stale and had constantly to be renewed; and while the incense arose two or three times a day, the heart could not but conceive of better things—viz., of incorruptible manna, and a perpetual arising from the heart of prayer and praise. One other thing beheld in this outer sanctuary suggested constantly the thought of something better beyond and to come, and that was the veil hiding from sight the holy of holies. Its presence and faintest movement spoke eloquently of something deeper and holier in the religious life. This veil is recognized by all in the regenerated life. They may refuse to go beyond it; but its presence is felt nevertheless, and it has a voice that speaks mysteriously in promise, rebuke, or encouragement according to the state of the soul. How a man can be content to live on this side of the veil, and not know the life beyond, is a wonder to men and angels. The reply is made that there is now no veil; that at Christ's death it was torn down, and all in the holy of holies is now seen, and we as a Church are living there. This is far from being so. Let the reader remember that the Gospel does not say that the veil was torn down, but rent. A rent veil is not removed. Moreover, the edges of a torn curtain come together and the things beyond are as well concealed as ever. Christ's death has made it possible for all to come into the holy of holies— namely, the experience of holiness. He has rent the curtain, but did not destroy it. The divided veil still hangs before the mysteries of sanctification, and it is a concealed life now as it has ever been. The advantage is that now, instead of one man entering once a year into the most holy place or life, behold! any one can come in. But while possible to all, it is not common to all. The veil is rent, but it is still there!

The second room, or inner sanctuary, stood for the sanctified life. What was there in the room that distinguished it from the other, and in a typical way differentiated it from regeneration?

The first thing realized on entering would be its deep quiet. The heavy folds of the drapery, the prohibition of human feet from its sacred precincts, the remoteness of the inner room from the other parts of the tabernacle and courts insured the stillness. The counterpart to this is found in the sanctified life. The instant we go behind the veil in the reception of the blessing a marvelous quiet and stillness of spirit settles upon us. We are in the secret place of the Most High. The restful life begins from that moment.

A second noticeable fact is that it was a hidden

place. No man could see the high priest through the veil, or dared to follow him. So the instant we are sanctified the vail drops behind us and we enter upon a hidden life. From that moment the world fails to understand us. Indeed, our own friends are thoroughly mystified. The expressions they use in their opinions and descriptions show how little they know of sanctification and the sanctified soul. It is a hidden life. Its motives, humility, joy, self-sacrifice, silence, and testimony are all misunderstood, and especially by the Church. It is a life so hidden that Satan makes woeful blunders in his temptations, and the sharp arrows of human hate fly wide of the mark, for the shooters do not know where the hidden soul is abiding.

Third, we mark the presence of angels. Truly when the heart is made pure our companionships become heavenly.

Fourth, we notice the ark. This ark typified the human heart. God's effort has ever been and is still to bring the heart into the holy of holies.

Fifth, we observe the two tables of the law in the ark. This is the very promise made concerning sanctification: that when that grace is given the law of God shall be " written in the mind and heart." Those two tables of law, one referring to God and the other to man, and written upon the soul, was only another way of saying that the man has perfect love.

Sixth, there is seen the bent attitude over the law. Study those intent faces and those bending forms and see an illustration of what takes place in the sanctified soul. Truly the Word of God is studied and pored over as never before.

Seventh, we mark the rod that bloomed, budded, and yielded almonds. Here is shown the perpetual fruitfulness of the sanctified life. Before being brought into the inner sanctuary the life was like a dry stick, but after that it not only bloomed and bore fruit, but did so continually.

Eighth, the incorruptible manna is seen. The heavenly bread was a blessing outside, but as the hours passed it melted or corrupted. Placed inside the ark in the most holy place, it remained always sweet and fresh. The contrast between this manna and the bread in the outer sanctuary, that had constantly to be replenished, is very striking, but not more so than a religious experience that melts and corrupts by twelve o'clock is different and inferior to one that abides sweet, fresh, and pure all the time.

Ninth, the mercy seat appears. From over the ark and underneath the wings of the bending angels God was accustomed to speak. And from a life in which we find God's law, abiding fruitfulness, and the perpetual manna, even Christ himself indwelling—from such a life God continues to speak. Some one has said: "God's most awful weapon is a holy man." Better far than great talents is a holy life. From such lips God speaks in warning, rebuke, comfort, and wondrous power. Such lives are mercy seats.

Tenth, we mark the abiding light. There was a peculiar radiance in the inner sanctuary. Neither sun, moon, nor stars shone in it, nor was there a lamp, as in the first room. A luminous glory filled the room, and it was abiding. No human hand was needed to replenish the invisible source. Unlike the lamp in the outer sanctuary, which burned high or low, this light continued as a steady, soft splendor all the while. The sanctified man understands this. From the fluctuating light of the regenerated life the soul goes into the steady, abiding radiance of sanctification. God supplies it and the soul revels in a sweet, inward spiritual day. From this time on one is guided peculiarly by the Spirit of God; and at the same time a wonderful independency of life springs up. Men may withdraw their lamps and candles, the sun may be hidden with the moon and stars; yet is there left within this wonderful spiritual light of holiness, and which is felt to be the glory of God.

Finally, there was the presence of God. Here was where Jehovah dwelt. "Thou that dwellest between the cherubim, shine forth." The glory of the blessing of sanctification is that it ushers the soul into the experience of the constant, conscious presence of God. He visits us in regeneration, but dwells in the soul in sanctification.

Who would not have Christ to be an indweller? If a visit is precious, how much more blessed to have him come in and take up his abode! This is what occurs when we pass from the outer room through the veil into the inner sanctuary. Heavenly spot! holy, quiet resting place of the soul! Here the light never goes out; and here the presence of God ever realized constitutes the balm, the consolation, and the glory of life.

CHAPTER VII.

THE SECOND APPROACH OF THE HIGH PRIEST TO THE TABERNACLE OR TEMPLE.

THERE were two approaches.

The first was a daily entrance into the outer sanctuary, preceded by cleansing at the laver and sprinkling of blood.

The second approach was made once a year, and was an approach to, and entrance within, the inner sanctuary, called the most holy place. This annual act on the part of the priest was enough to arouse thought then, and should do so now. Yet there are countless Christians who have read of this deeply solemn scene and failed to realize its typical teaching. If it does not establish the fact of a second approach to God, a second revelation to the soul, a second experience distinct and clear from regeneration, and deeper as an experience in holiness of heart and life, as the inner sanctuary transcended the outer, then we have a symbol in the Bible not yet understood.

It is wonderful how the doctrine of a second work of grace makes this symbolic approach all luminous and powerful. We call attention to some

4   (49)

of the facts connected with this second approach
to, and entrance into, the holy of holies.

One feature is the rarity of entrance. One man
only entered, and he but once a year. Thus rarely
the blessing of sanctification was enjoyed in the
Old Testament dispensation; while the number
who enter now, as compared with those who do not
seek the inner life of holiness, is actually, in disparity, as one is to a multitude. Not that it is to
remain thus; the Scriptures prophesy differently;
and the people already are waking up to their
privileges and are pressing through the rent veil
into the life of holiness.

The multitude gazed after the priest when he
disappeared in the sanctuary. And so to-day if
there is anything that arouses the attention of the
people it is when some man or woman of God goes
beyond the veil into the hidden, unknown life of
holiness. Little is said about a man's regeneration, but the whole community is interested in this
second approach to God.

The people remained praying without while the
priest was within. And well they might, for if
ever a man was in danger he was on that day.
Certain acts on his part meant swift and certain
death. And so the people prayed; and so they
need to pray now when a man starts to enter the

inner sanctuary of grace beyond the veil. That such a man is in a critical state no one who has any knowledge of the doctrine and experience of sanctification will dream of denying. If he fails to enter, he will never be the same man again. Death of a certain nature is certain to befall him. Let the people pray for such an one as he approaches the veil of the most holy place.

The priest cleansed himself. Clean before, there is an additional purification before entering this inner shrine. The teaching is that while regeneration is in a sense cleanness, yet is there another personal cleansing before obtaining the greatest blessing God has to bestow upon us. Under increased light things are revealed that were not before noticed. These have to be laid aside, while the indwelling, inherited uncleanness of depravity is recognized and likewise offered up. This truth is verified by Christ's own words to his disciples, "Now ye are clean through the word;" but a few verses after he prays, "Father, sanctify them." Clean, and yet needing a second and deeper purification! This divine cleansing is sought by a personal cleansing, the separation from body, mind, and soul of everything questionable and defiling. Before the priest went into the most holy place he cleansed himself; before the child of God enters into this blessed experience of sanctification he first purifies himself as far as human power can do. Tobacco, snuff, stimulants, narcotics, secret societies, questionable businesses, all go.

The priest laid aside his splendid robes and attired himself in plain linen garments. Aside from the fact of the white linen standing for purity, there is a suggestion here in regard to dress. Somehow I notice that people in gorgeous apparel do not get within the veil. Splendid robes or the showy garment is hardly the proper garb in which to wait on God for the attainment of a humble, Christlike heart.

The priest went alone. No one could go with him. So, in seeking the blessing of sanctification, the experience from the beginning to the end is one of profound solitariness. The soul is drawn away into the wilderness to meet its Beloved; the man goes "without the camp bearing his reproach;" there is a lonely lifting up on the cross and a lonely dying on the cross. When Jacob sought this blessing he sent his family across the brook and remained alone with God. When the writer sought it he had to seek, pray, and groan alone. When the reader seeks it he will have to consent to go without his friends, without his family, and without his congregation and Church. The sanctifying blood, both in the Old and New Testament times, in the time of Moses and the time of Christ, in the Jewish and in the Christian day, is always " outside the gate " and " without the camp." The priest went in alone to see God in his holiness. We must do the same. The questions are: Are we willing to go alone? can we stand solitariness?

The priest took the blood with him. The teaching that leaps out of this fact is that to come into the life and experience of holiness we must come with the blood of Christ. God tells us in this that sanctification as a blessing is not growth, not a development; but an obtainment through the blood. The priest had already sprinkled himself with blood in order to enter the outer sanctuary; but, mark you, he is required to bring the blood the second time in order to obtain entrance into the most holy place. The two blood carryings or sprinklings show beyond question two works of Christ, two accomplishments of grace, and two distinct exercises of faith upon the part of the soul. He who seeks holiness or sanctification by development, growth, or any other way save by faith in the blood of Christ, will be inevitably doomed to disappointment and failure.

The scene of Cain rejected amid his fruits, and Abel accepted with the blood of the lamb is still being beheld in the Church to-day. How slow men are to learn that all of the spiritual life is of grace! Paul had trouble here with one of his churches: " O foolish Galatians, who hath be- witched you? . . . This only would I learn of you, Received ye the Spirit by the works of the law, or by the hearing of faith? Are ye so foolish? having begun in the Spirit, ARE YE NOW MADE PER- FECT BY THE FLESH?" My brother, cease trying to grow into holiness; take the blood with you, and the veil will open to receive you. This second appli- cation of blood is an unanswerable argument and proof of a second work of grace received by faith.

The reappearance of the priest meant blessing for the people. He went in and prevailed for them, and comes forth again with blessings for all.

And so is it to this day. Whoever goes behind the veil, whoever seeks and obtains the blessing of a pure heart, will appear again among the people, and this time with wonderfully multiplied power to do them good. He will be antagonized in many directions; but O the power he has with God, and the power he has over souls to quicken, encourage, and lead them to God for salvation! How tender and gentle with men! how fearless of men and devils and the world! how bold for the truth and Christ! He has looked in the face of God, and can now look calmly and properly upon the face of man; he has the tongue of fire and his words burn—he indeed burns while he utters them; he has the fullness of the blessing and overflows; he has a mighty propelling force in him, a fire in his bones, a love in his heart that will not let him rest until the salvation of God appears and abides.

The Lord sent the disciples behind the veil at Pentecost, and they reappeared to bless the world. Madam Guyon and Lady Havergal went into the inner sanctuary and came back to bless France and England. Wesley and some of his early preachers and workers, Clarke, Benson, Fletcher, and Carvosso, all went into the most holy place and came back with shining faces, burning tongues, and blessings for their race.

Finney and Inskip went within the veil and came back filled, thrilled, and fired, and before they left this world for heaven filled hundreds of silent churches with songs and praises, made many unhappy homes happy, and brought thousands of immortal souls to God.

He that goes behind the veil into the holy experience of sanctification and comes back will reappear to bless the people. He has only to tell of

what he saw within the veil, the perpetual light and
glory and holy stillness, the incorruptible manna,
and the constant presence of God—and God himself will take care of the testimony and will answer it as by fire from heaven on the burning
hearts of the listeners.

CHAPTER VIII.

THE TWO CROSSINGS.

APART of this chapter appears in the author's work called "Sanctification," but for the sake of strengthening and perfecting the argument on symbolism it is transcribed and enlarged here. For suggestions in this striking symbol lesson the writer made acknowledgment in his former work.

The second blessing is seen in the two crossings made by the children of Israel: one over the Red Sea, the other over the river Jordan. As the two crossings took place under the special direction of God, and as they were so markedly different, it stands to reason that they were typical of different spiritual truths and experiences. He that educated and prepared us for the sacrifice and death of Christ by the lamb taken from the fold, slain in the afternoon, eaten with bitter herbs, with no bones broken, and resting on a spit the shape of a cross; he who taught the resurrection by the miracle of Jonah's life, and his own descent from heaven, with the satisfying and sustaining power of his life, by the manna that fell from the skies,

(57)

would surely typify and symbolize so wonderful a
blessing as sanctification in some striking and
forcible way. The two crossings are thus intended
of God. The passage at the Red Sea teaches all
that occurs at conversion, and the passage at the
river Jordan illustrates sanctification. The contrast between the two is marked.

At the Red Sea the Israelites were fleeing from
an enemy, and were delivered; at the Jordan
they were not in flight, but were drawn by the
goodness and beauty of the land of Canaan, and
entered into rest.

As a sinner a man has much to dread, but what
has the child of God to flee from? No sermon of
threatening or terrifying character can move the
regenerated man toward the experience of holiness.
He feels the blood and realizes that he is safe.
The argument or appeal that stirs him is a Canaan
life that surpasses in its rest, plenty, and victory
anything that he has known since he left Egypt.
Driven at the Red Sea of pardon, he must be
drawn at the Jordan of holiness. Spears pushed
him into the first experience, but milk and honey
must draw him into the second.

Again, at the Red Sea the children of Israel
were in great haste, while at the Jordan we see
evidence of calm and deliberate action. This

again strikingly brings out the two blessings. Conversion is found in a hurry, but the blessing of sanctification comes invariably after deep reflection and full deliberation and conclusion of mind.

Conviction for sin strikes the unconverted like a cyclone, but conviction for holiness steals into the Christian heart like a gentle breath from heaven. The latter is not alarmed like the sinner, but melted. He is not in despair, but humbled to the dust as he is made to see the dark principle of sin abiding within. He turns the matter over, he searches his heart afresh, he examines his relations with God, every step showing deliberation.

Again, at the Red Sea the Israelites went down into the sea a multitude of empty-handed and unarmed fugitives; but at the Jordan they went in fully armed. How clearly appears here the state of the flying penitent seeking safety, and the consecrated Christian coming with all his powers to God, seeking a life of perfect rest and holiness!

What does a poor sinner have to bring to God? He is an undone rebel asking for mercy. But the child of God comes with a heart full of love and life full of service for his Lord. He has done many things for which he has felt within the " well done, good and faithful servant.'' He is not a flying transgressor suing for pardon, but an approved child of God asking for perfect likeness to the God he loves,

Again, at the Red Sea the children of Israel stepped into a dry and open path between the waters—not a wave or pool was left in their course; but at the Jordan they had to place their feet in the water before the waves receded and the path became open.

This most strikingly illustrates the entrance upon the two lives of regeneration and sanctification. In the way of pardon the path is clear; we flee through prayer into the experience. At such a time we are weak and could not stand any difficulty flung before us; but, in obtaining the blessing of sanctification, our faith is naturally much stronger, and so the way is not open at first; we actually have to put our feet into the waves before they recede. In other words, we claim the blessing by a strong faith before there is an indication or assurance of the great salvation. In a very special manner here the faith precedes the work and the witness.

Still again, there is seen a great difference in the emotional life after the two crossings. At the Red Sea the Israelites were in transports. They sung, they danced, they struck the timbrel, and the burden of their song was their deliverance from the Egyptians. But it was a short-lived joy. It soon gave way to murmuring. At the Jordan there seems to have been an unutterable sense of peace, a calm, holy joy and triumph. As you read the description you cannot but feel the in· tense but voiceless emotion of the multitudes. It was an hour too blessed and holy for noisy cymbals. The memories of the past, the recollec- tion of the mistakes and wanderings for forty years, the remembrance that triumph had been offered them long before, the tender mindfulness of the pity and long-suffering of God meanwhile, to- gether with the overpowering thought that " Ca- naan, sweet Canaan," so long wished for and sought after, was at last theirs, contributed to an experience so tender, so melting, and so overpow- ering that the desire was rather to sit or stand still in the presence of God in a holy triumph too deep for earthly language to express. But from that time began the real joy-life of this people. Grum- bling and murmuring gave way to shouts of con- stant victory.

In conversion the timbrel is frequently brought forth. Miriam takes the floor; but often the writer has noticed the gusty and ephemeral exist- ence of the emotions of that hour. The tongue, alas! learns soon to murmur. And the proof that

the joy seems not to remain appears from testimonies given by the regenerated when they make
reference to the time when ten, twenty, forty
years ago, they were so happy. They talk as if it
was the soul's privilege to be full of joy only once
in a lifetime.

Sanctification is a deeper experience than conversion. It involves a perfect surrender, an abso·
lute and final consecration, and the utter extermina-
tion of sin in the heart. Naturally we would look
for great demonstrations. And so it is in the case
of a great many, and especially when God is
pleased to call attention to the doctrine in certain
skeptical communities.

But sometimes the crossing of the Jordan of the
death of self into the Canaan of life is marked by
a joy that seems too profound for words; it is an
experience full of glory, but unutterable. A peace
enters that spreads, deepens, and sweetens as it
goes until the entire nature is filled and thrilled
with it.

A sense of unmistakable fullness is realized.
The consciousness fills one that every part of the
soul and body has been reached. A sense of being inwardly healed, an exquisite experience of
purity is felt, while the soul fairly melts with a
baptism of perfect love; and through it all and in

it all the Spirit of God whispers to the soul: " This is sanctification."

This sometimes takes place with little outward demonstration. The wind has leveled the wave. But the joy-life has begun; and it is a joy that is full and that remains. It is not Arabia, but Canaan that has been entered, and Joshua is happier than Miriam.

While a life of hard-fought battles is entered upon, yet there is a constant experience of glorious victories. Grumbling has been removed by shouting, and murmuring by praises. The desert wandering is over, there is a blessed entrance upon rest, while the soul is rejoicing in a land flowing with milk and honey, " where the flowers bloom forever, and the sun is always bright."

And so the peace of God—not peace *with* God (for that stands for the experience of pardon as shown in Rom. v. 1), but *of* God—bathes the soul, like the light falls continually and eternally upon the hills of heaven.

It is a peculiar peace. It is the peace of sanctification. You will know it by the features mentioned. But aside from that you will recognize it by the voice of the Sanctifier, who is enshrined within saying: " Child, you are clean."

CHAPTER IX.

THE LOVE SLAVE; OR, THE TWO KINDS OF SERVICE.

THAT there should be two kinds of service rendered God strikes the mind with surprise. That there is such a thing is plainly taught in the terms "servants" and "friends" used by Christ, and is especially clear in Exodus xxi. 1–6, from which we draw the suggestions that appear in this chapter.

In this passage one man is seen in two relations with his Master: first as a bond servant, and second as a love slave. As a bond servant he stands for the regenerated man. The fact that he had been bought, that his life was one of service, and that he at the end of six years was free to leave his master is a most faithful picture of the regenerated life. One of the most startling things brought out in the passage and tallying with the experience is this strange power in the converted life to " go out free " from the Master, a fact that finds a dreadful echo in the disposition at times to leave God, and which disposition or tendency we find recognized in our hymn book, and notably in the lines:

> Prone to wander, Lord, I feel it!
> Prone to leave the God I love.

Before this power and tendency in one of his disciples Christ at the last supper sat, it may be reverently said, powerless, his only words being: "What thou doest, do quickly." After being in the service of the Lord for over three years Judas was free to leave, and did leave!

In the passage in Exodus we see the bond servant suddenly becoming a love slave. The reader will notice that the service of the slave to the master is not interrupted nor ended, but simply changed in its character to a higher form of service. He has been a servant for years, and doubtless received wages, but has now come to the moment where, by his own will and act, he alters his relation to his master in the profoundest way. He is the same man, but in a new relation. As a love slave, he represents the sanctified man. We know of no place in the Bible where the change from the regenerated to the sanctified life is taught more beautifully or powerfully.

First, the bond servant made a voluntary gift of himself to his master. Here appears that solemn dedication and perfect consecration of self to God

5

that precedes the blessing of sanctification. Some
say this was done in seeking pardon of sin. But not
so; a sinner has no thought of consecration, and
nothing indeed to consecrate. What has he but
sins? He is a rebel crying to God for mercy, and
obtains it by dropping his sins and believing on
the Lord Jesus Christ. There is not a word in
the Bible about a sinner consecrating. The sinner
surrenders; the Christian consecrates. The sinner
gives up his sins; the Christian gives up himself.
The first leads to regeneration; the second, to sanctification.

Secondly, it was an eternal gift. He said he
would serve him forever. The trouble with those
failing to obtain the blessing of holiness is right
here. They have mental reservations, they leave
loopholes for escape, they will not finally and forever surrender the whole life and man to God.
Hence they fail to find the " more excellent way."
The man who obtains the blessing does like the
bond servant, signs himself away to God forever,
no matter what God gives or withholds, what he
does or does not do.

Thirdly, he enters on a love service. He that
doubts there are two kinds of service, let him study
awhile the difference between a faithful servant
and a devoted wife. The one with all his faithful-

ness looks for wages; the other only asks for love. Then tell me whose step is the softest and swiftest in time of sickness, whose hand the gentlest, whose eye the most watchful, and who is speediest in anticipating and meeting every want. The fact apparent with many Christians is that they serve God for wages. Some take their pay in the respectability and social standing Christianity gives; others live for experiences, states, and spiritual consolations. Withdraw these, and they fall away at once. Some serve just to keep free from the lash of conscience and rebuke of God. When a man gets sanctified he serves God for the sake of God himself. He becomes a love slave. He reads the Bible, prays in secret, and goes to church with an enjoyment of these things scarcely dreamed of before. He talks for Christ and works for him, not perfunctorily, but gladly, joyously for his own sake. He asks no reward but his constant, loving presence. He gives up the smile of men, the rewards of earth, the promotions and dignities even of the Church. His only request and desire is: "Give me Jesus." Sanctification makes a love slave out of the servant of God.

Fourthly, he feels free to stay. It looks like a life of hopeless bondage to the world; but while there is a law in it, it is the " law of liberty." So delightful is the new relation he would not leave it. He feels free, but free to stay. The disposition to wander and leave is gone. He is like the peasant who requested the angel of death to call for a him at the door of heaven after he had been there a week to see whether he desired to return to earth. The answer to the knock at the door was the glad cry, "Satisfied!" Free, but free not to leave, but to stay. This is sanctification.

Fifthly, the blessing is obtained by the death route. The bond servant was brought to the door post and his ear bored through with an awl. The cross and the nail is at once brought to view in symbol. To become a love slave or sanctified man, the old man has to die on the cross. Many are seeking holiness by a palace car route, by the rocking chair and good book method, by the meditative and self-repressive way; but the true and only route is the death route.

Then many who accept the idea of the death of self as necessary for the obtainment of the blessing crave to die in ways attractive and pleasing to men and agreeable to themselves. It is impossible! There is no form of dissolution that is pleasant to look upon. There is no death, from a worm to a whale, that is pleasing to the sight. A dying man is a solemnizing and painful spectacle, although he does not know it, nor does he think or care how he looks. People do not come to that hour with curled hair, painted cheeks, gem-be-decked ears, and elaborate toilet. These things are forgotten and despised in the hour of death.

When the " old man " is being crucified, or in other words, when the man seeking holiness is dy-ing to sin, and to the flesh, and to the world, with all its favors, rewards, opinions, and persecutions, he is not attractive to the world, and to many in the Church he has no comeliness or beauty that any should desire him. He is dying at the altar, stripped, shunned, laughed at, misunderstood, and unknown as his Lord died on the cross. He be-comes indifferent and then oblivious to it all. He loses sight of the crowd, thinks of and seeks Christ alone, " sinks into the purple flood " out of sight of friend and foe, and rises into the blessed, indescribable life of God. "I am crucified with Christ: nevertheless I live; yet not I, but Christ liveth in me."

Sixthly, he gets reproach. There was no doubt that the servant whose ear was bored was pointed out in derision. The mark in the ear and this vol-untary, perpetual slavehood brought upon him both jest and condemnation. If any man wants to know what the " reproach of Christ" means, what the " offense of the cross " is, let him get sanctified.

The unmistakable marks of sanctification and the life itself will awaken speedily and constantly both smile and sneer, ridicule and opposition. We do not stop to explain why this is so, but simply mention the fact.

Seventhly, he becomes a marked servant of God. The ear of the servant was bored so that all men looking upon him knew who and what he was. In the South you can tell a man's cattle by a mark, and his cotton bales by a brand. There need be and is no confusion. Often we have felt the need of a mark that would distinguish the Church from the world. As it is, all know how difficult it is to tell the difference between many who profess to be Christ's and those who know him not. Sanctifition supplies the mark. When a man gets the blessing of holiness he can be recognized in any crowd or place as belonging to Christ; his "speech betrayeth him," his life shows that he "has been with Jesus," he "bears in his body the marks of the Lord Jesus."

Eighthly, it is a fixed experience or life. Bore a man's ear to the door, and he is a fixture. Nail a man to the cross, and there he is. This is the blessed peculiarity of the sanctified: you know where to find them. They need not be sought at questionable places and gatherings, nor in the opera, theater, and ballroom, but always at and by the cross. Wherever you find the cross of Christ there will you find the sanctified. He is nailed to it.

Ninthly, he comes into deepest intimacy and honor with the master. Any one can see that when a servant refused freedom offered him, and voluntarily consigned himself to a life of perpetual service to his former master, this act not only dignified and ennobled the servant, but secured him a place in the esteem, confidence, and affection of the master and family of the most exalted nature. It would be difficult to describe the intimacy and union, the tenderness and power of the relation thus established.

So it is in sanctification. To become God's love slave means a union and communion that no pen can describe nor tongue express. When a person makes the full and eternal surrender of self to God that is involved in sanctification, it truly seems that from that time God withholds nothing from that soul; the cup is kept full, the head anointed, the table spread in the presence of enemies, the windows of heaven opened, and such blessings poured out that there is not room enough to contain them.

CHAPTER X.

THE HOLY OIL.

THIS symbol appears in Exodus xxx. 23–33. The "blood" always stands for Christ and his work, and the "oil" for the work of the Holy Ghost. God calls it the "holy ointment" and "anointing oil." As a symbol it strikingly sets forth the blessing of sanctification, or holiness. We call attention to some things about it that places its meaning beyond all doubt.

It was made under divine direction. Holiness is no humanly devised affair. It is not the product of a heated brain or the ravings or wild imaginations of a fanatic; it is of the Lord. He, so to speak, compounded and gave us the blessing.

It was very costly. Let the reader glance at the Scripture and see how many shekels it required for the preparation of the holy oil. Then let him recall what it cost to give the Church the blessing of holiness. Think of the life, suffering, groans, tears, bloody sweat, and death of the Son of God. Paul said He suffered without the gate that he might sanctify the people. Truly this blessing at which so many are sneering to-day cost an infinite price.

(72)

It was very fragrant. The myrrh, calamus, and cinnamon combined made a most delightful odor. But it was not as fragrant as holiness itself. Think of perfect love, perfect peace, perfect faith, and perfect joy all poured into a purified heart. The fragrance of such a life soon steals through the home, is felt in the Church, distributes itself through the community, and even goes round the world. The spices of Ceylon can be smelled leagues away at sea; but the perfume of a holy life crosses seas and lands, belts the world, and even after hundreds of years is as fragrant as the first day it started forth to bless mankind.

It was never to be placed on a stranger; it was for the ·Israelite. So sanctification is not for the unconverted, but for the regenerated. This is the blessing Christ came to bring to his people.

It was not put on the flesh. The flesh stands for carnality, and not until the child of God renounces it, and by a mental act dooms it to death, does the oil of holiness fall upon him.

It was put on the blood. In Leviticus xiv. 14–20 a full description is given. Let the reader turn back to the chapter that describes " The Two Anointings " to see it fully explained. Suffice it to say that in the cleansing of a man he was first anointed with blood, and afterward with the holy oil.

The oil was put on the blood; not simultaneously, but subsequently. Here is plainly seen the second blessing. So on the blood-washed disciples came the anointing of the Holy Ghost on the day of Pentecost. So with the Ephesian disciples and with Cornelius. So has it been since and will ever be. The blood-washed may look for the baptism of the Holy Ghost. The blood; after that, the oil.

It was never to be imitated. Alas that any one should try! But every converted man who insists that regeneration is sanctification, that what he obtained at pardon is what others have obtained in sanctification, such a man is imitating the holy oil. Whenever an unsanctified man thrusts forward his experience before men, and claims to have what the illumined mind can see he has not, the oil is being imitated. God pronounced death on any one imitating the holy oil of Israel. And judgments descend to-day from heaven upon those who confuse God's people and call a creation of their own, the defective experience of an untempered heart, the blessing of holiness which God sends upon the consecrated heart in answer to faith.

This holy oil that appears in the passage in Exodus did some things. It made holy. This is the statement of the twenty-ninth verse. In Leviticus the word "clean" is used. Let the reader look well here. It is not until the oil is placed upon the blood, a subsequent work, that the person is said to be clean or holy.

It prepares for service. This was so true that Christ told the disciples to tarry in Jerusalem until they had received it. After it came upon them the whole world knows how these anointed men flew to the work of saving the human race.

It is amazing how devoted and tireless and successful in soul saving a Christian becomes after he has had the oil of holiness poured upon him.

It ends friction. We have no lack of machinery, men, and methods in the Church to-day. This is not the trouble. The trouble is slowness, creaking, complaining, friction. O for a baptism of the holy oil! How swiftly, easily, and delightfully everything would then run. The writer affirms this not only from the spectacle given us in the book of Acts of the apostolic Church after the baptism of the Holy Ghost had descended, but from what he has beheld for two years in the church of which he was pastor. He has also noticed that there is no religious gathering that runs so easily, powerfully, successfully, and with such utter absence of friction as a holiness meeting. The holy oil is the explanation.

It makes the face to shine. Whenever the holy oil comes upon the heart the countenance is transfigured. When Moses got it he had to put a veil over his face. When the reader obtains the anointing the shadows and darkness of his face will be bound to go, under the drippings of that oil that brightens and glorifies the countenance.

It means healing. The trouble in the Church to-day is the number of the spiritually sick and wounded. Invalids are seen on every side. We feel the need of wards named according to the ailments of Church members. Let the people obtain the second blessing, or the oil of holiness, and the Church invalids will at once disappear and the wards be uninhabited. The blessing of sanctification heals the heart. Chronic complaints end, all tongue diseases vanish, and fretfulness and fault finding disappear with the plague of inbred sin which sanctification casts out. The man is well and whole and ready for the work and service of God at all times.

It is preparation for death. Christ said about Mary: "She hath anointed me for my burial." When we obtain the blessing of sanctification we are ready for death, burial, and the judgment. Reason tells us that there should be such a grace or blessing. In a world of falling trees, burning vessels, colliding trains, and flying pistol bullets, we need a constant preparation of heart and readiness to end life and see God. God has not overlooked our need nor left unsupplied our want. There is a blessing subsequent to regeneration typified by the holy oil that when received fits us as never before for life and also keeps us continually ready for death and the coming of the Son of Man. Methodist preachers a hundred years ago had the blessing and were known to be ready to preach a sermon or to die at a moment's warning. A good many of them to-day require more time in each event. But whoever has the oil, whether he be in the pulpit or pew, is willing at any time to pray, preach, and testify for God, and is ready at any hour or moment to be summoned into the presence of his Lord.

Would that every reader could say that the "oil" is now on the "blood;" that he has received the anointing of the Holy One!

CHAPTER XI.

THE TWO WAYS.

IT was a long time before the writer discovered that there were two ways in the spiritual life leading to heaven. Not two ways leading in different directions, and that are contrary to each other, but both pointing and leading harmoniously. But if both lead to eternal life, what need for two distinct ways? The answer is found in observing that one way is within the other way. Here is the mystery of the gospel.

One is a highway; and regeneration is a highway. The tendency with many has been to depreciate the new birth, but the teaching of the word of God is that it is a highway. "Whosoever is born of God sinneth not." Certainly this is an elevated life. The truly converted man living up to his privileges should not commit sin.

In the highway is a way; and this last is called by Isaiah " the way of holiness." Let the reader mark well that the prophet does not say the highway, but the way, is the way of holiness. This second way that does not appear at the first glance is the one so deeply interesting to us now,

and not only to us, but to a great multitude in the
land beside. The interest is deepening all the
while, and members in all the Churches are arous-
ing themselves to inquire about this other way,
that is so mysteriously mentioned as being in the
highway. What if it be that " narrow way " with
the " straight gate," about which Christ says:
" Few there be that find it?" Anyhow, it is a way
of life and grace, and it is for all, whether they
will enter or not, and so we should all examine
into it, not being turned aside by the voice of ridicule or prejudice.

About this way of holiness appears several
things, according to Isaiah's description.

It is in the highway. The teaching is that in
the regenerated life is to be found the second
blessing, or way of holiness.

It is also a hidden way. It is so concealed in
the eighth vers and thirty-fifth chapter of Isaiah
that many read it for years before seeing that
two ways are mentioned, and that it is the second way and not the first that is called the way of
holiness. So as a religious experience, holiness
is so hidden in regeneration that there are many
to-day who cannot and will not believe in its existence. The reasons for this concealment can be
found in the wisdom of God, the best method of

dealing with souls, and the darkening power
which inbred sin, left in the regenerated heart, has
upon the spiritual understanding. God has hidden the blessing as he hides the most precious
things of the earth, and as he concealed behind
the second veil the deeper and more sacred mysteries of his kingdom. And men live and die in
ignorance of the life and way of holiness because
they are unwilling to put forth the same energy
and toil to obtain the hidden wealth of grace that
many are glad to do to procure the gems and gold
and riches buried in the ground. There are out-
croppings enough from the soil to invite investigation; there are glimpses of the way obtained now
and then, sufficient to woo any soul to its complete
discovery; but some men for certain reasons do
not press on and in, and so the Way of Holiness
remains hidden and unknown.

It is a clean way. Isaiah says: " Nothing unclean shall pass over it "—that is, we have to
" cleanse ourselves from all filthiness of the flesh
and spirit "—an act of our own—before we can step
into this way. There is a sanctifying of self which
precedes the sanctifying work of God. Here is
the explanation of the failure of many. There is
some bosom sin, secret ambition, questionable
habit, or reluctance to yield to the will of God in

everything, that keeps them out. Of course they cannot enter in with wrong things in the heart; of course the Holy Spirit will not descend upon a pile of unsurrendered carnality. It is a clean way, and in it we keep clean all the time. This is its charm and glory. All who walk in the way of holiness rejoice in a grace that keeps the soul white and pure every moment. In the physical life the eyelid with regular, periodic movement keeps the ball clean; but in the way of holiness there is the thrilling experience of a continuous touch and application of the purifying grace of God, so that the soul is pure all the time and evermore. Every housewife knows what a gathering and accumulation of soiled linen there is in a week's time; then comes the wash day and the restoration of lost whiteness to the garments. But what if there could be a process of keeping the garments clean all the time? This discovery, thanks be to God, is made in regard to our spiritual garments in the way of holiness. There is a marvelous soiling of garments in the average Christian life; and there are regular wash days almost unconsciously settled upon. The end of the day, the coming Sabbath, the protracted meeting, and the annual camp meeting are the favorite wash days with many of God's people.

6

And blessed times they are; and many defiled
garments are made pure and white once more.
But in the way of holiness these periodic wash
days are done away with.   It is a clean way and
keeps us clean.   Nothing impure passes over it.
There has been found a blessing which constantly
touches with its holy, whitening, cleansing power
every thought of the mind, word of the mouth,
act of the life—yes, better and deeper still—keeps
the heart pure, so that we walk with God in white,
in conscious cleanness of soul every moment of
our existence.

It is a way filled with the divine Presence.   The
margin reads: "He shall be with them."   Here,
again, is a distinguishing characteristic of this
way.   The presence of God is always felt in conscious, or, as á Kempis would say, in "recollect-
ed" moments.   He may not be in the mind every
moment, but he is with and in the soul all the
same.   There is no need to look out and abroad
for him.   He is always within.

It is a plain way.   "A wayfaring man, though a
fool, need not err therein."   A fool can find it.
Hidden from the doubter and the scoffer and the
spiritually proud and shallow, yet it is so plain
that if any man really wants a pure heart he can
find the blessing.   He may be poor, obscure, un-

lettered, even simple-minded, but he can get it. God in his wisdom hid the way of holiness from the wise and prudent who did not care to pay the price, or comply with the humbling conditions of holiness; but the same God in mercy makes the way manifest to the poor and humble in spirit who pant after the whole image and full salvation of Christ in the soul. Suppose God had made access to the way of holiness along the line of attainment instead of obtainment; suppose only scholars could have met the conditions. Instead of that, instead of lifting the requisition high, he has put it down, so that the children, young people, sick people, old people, weary-hearted people —yes, even fools—can find it.

It is a safe way. " No lion shall be there." This is a remarkable statement. It doesn't say there will be no lions, but no lions will be there! They will be seen and heard, but will not be in the way of holiness. There will be many enemies, with the rage of lions, but they will not be able to rend or even touch us. There is a secret place, a surely kept life, and it is in the way of holiness, where we are strongly and amazingly protected from the hate, wrath, tongues, and hands of men. The arrow comes short, the poison proves harmless, and while men look for us to drop down

dead, behold, we shake the beast off into the fire
and go on unharmed and unmoved. One has to
come into the blessing before he can understand
the marvelous deliverance. Truly, it is a safe
way. Men can tear the reputation to pieces, but
the character remains, which is far more important, together with patience, purity, perfect love,
and the unchanging peace of God. Men may exhaust their ingenuity in methods of attack and
slander, and yet the soul will live, love, and work
on just the same. The writer has seen the moon
floating in cloudless beauty in spite of thousands
of barking dogs in farmyard, village, and city.
Listen to them! What an uproar! Now look at
the moon! We can conceive of men shooting arrows, firing guns, and throwing stones at the quiet,
unanswering orb; but far aloft and away in the
tranquil depths of heaven she shines on and moves
on untouched and undisturbed. Such an uplifted,
serene, and unmoved life, thank God, is the privilege and experience of every truly sanctified
soul.

It is a joyful way. They who walk in it have
songs and everlasting joy. One of the remarkable
features of holiness is its singing spirit, and another, its gladness. The holiness songs can be
recognized by their triumphant and joyful charac-

ter. The shouts and cries born of conscious freedom, purity, and victory run through them all.
There is a great joy springing up and running
over in the sanctified heart. And it is an everlasting joy. The cause is abiding and so the joy
remains. They as a people cannot keep from being demonstrative, any more than a spring can
keep from running over at its brim. People look
on, surprised and mystified at the shining faces,
clapping hands, and rapturous shouts of holiness
meetings. They themselves are in the "highway" and do not feel so inclined to praise the
Lord. They forget that the everlasting joy and
singing which Isaiah speaks of is *not* in the highway, but *in the way of holiness.* Let them get
into the "way," and that mysterious gladness
which so puzzled them as witnessed in other persons will at once gush up in their own breasts.
Just as, when the great auger bores through the
last strata of rock and gravel, the artesian water
springs and leaps up high in the air, thus instantly,
when a perfect consecration has bored its way
through everything, and we step into the way of
holiness, will joy burst forth and gush upward in
the soul, never to cease its sweet, clear, beautiful
upspringing forever.

It is an unmistakably religious way. Those in

it are seen coming to Zion. Whatever is said about sanctified people, it is a noticeable fact that no one accuses them of being worldly. Their faces are not toward the world, but are set steadfastly to go to Jerusalem.

It is an obtainable way. The word used in the tenth verse is " obtain." There is a great difference between attain and obtain. A man struggling through a lifetime for a fortune at last attains his desire, but what years of pain and toil slumber under the word " attain!" Another man, without a stroke of pen or ax, quietly inherits a great fortune from his father. His case is one of obtainment. What a contrast to the other! How much easier to obtain than attain! For fourteen years the writer tried by prayer and Christian works to attain the blessing of a pure heart, or holiness, and constantly failed, for it is not to be had that way. At last, learning that it was a matter of inheritance through the death of Christ, he probated his case by faith in the Court of Grace, and obtained in a moment the unspeakable gift; and ever since has been walking in the way of holiness toward Zion, with everlasting joy on his head and glory in his soul.

CHAPTER XII.

THE TWO COVENANTS.

MEN are accustomed to speak of the "three dispensations" as if they found these terms in the Word of God. Mr. Fletcher grows eloquent in his attempt to divide the religious life into three periods, corresponding to what he calls the dispensations of the Father, Son, and Holy Ghost. Writers also, in recognizing the Patriarchal, Mosaic, and Christian ages of the world, try to manufacture three states of grace or soul life to agree with the pet theory mentioned above. The Bible is perfectly silent about three states of grace or three moral periods or three dispensations. But while silent here, it has much to say of two covenants—sometimes calling them the old and new, and at other times the first and second. These two covenants embrace all that God does for the soul on earth, and accurately describe the two works of grace, regeneration and sanctification. Let men rid their minds of the man-manufactured spiritual terms of three dispensations and fix their attention on the God-spoken words of two covenants, and begin to see what each contained; and

(87)

the result will be a marvelous clearing up of the
shadows that rest upon some of our doctrines and
a blessed revealment of a second work of grace
contained in the second covenant.

The First Covenant.—This began in Eden and
swept its arch of grace over patriarchs, prophets,
priests, and kings, and properly ended on the
morning of Pentecost.   Under this covenant lived
and died Adam, Abraham, Moses, David, Elijah,
Malachi, John the Baptist, and our blessed Lord
himself.   Patriarchal simplicity of worship was
changed to the more ornate and spectacular Levitical rites, but they were both under the first covenant.   The prophets spoke of a covenant to come
of remarkable character, but they all died under
the first without beholding the second.   The
Saviour was born under the first, coming not to
destroy but to fulfill.   He met its requirements,
answered the types, kept every feast, deposed not
a single priest, died and arose from the dead still
under its blessing, and not until ten days after his
ascension into heaven did he set up the second
covenant.   What has been called the second dispensation, or the dispensation of the Son, is really
Christ obedient to the first covenant, preparing
the Church for the second.

In the first covenant we find much of ritual

and ceremony. We find, however, justification
and regeneration. Men not only possessed religion, but enjoyed it. There was much of spiritual
consolation, and one need not go beyond the
Psalms and other books in the Old Testament to
find the most suitable and fervent expression of
religious emotion and condition. We find, also,
great liberality in gifts to God, and lives that
moved under God's protecting and delivering care.

But the first covenant was not faultless. This
is God's statement in Hebrews, and completely an-
swers the objection made to a second work of
grace in the plea that God does everything perfectly and completely in one work. The first
covenant was not faultless, says the Word of God,
and mentions some of the faults. One was that it
did not purge the worshiper of sin. It secured
the pardon of sin, but not its purging or elimina-
tion. There is a difference between sins of actual
transgression and sin as an indwelling nature or
principle. Paul calls the last named the " body
of sin." Let it be remembered that purging is
removing, not pardoning. Under the first covenant the body of sin was not purged. A second
fault was that there was a " constant remembrance
of sin." The regenerated man knows well the
meaning and force of this expression. A third

fault was that under this covenant the " comer " could not be " made perfect.'' Here allusion is made to the very work of grace which gives character and glory to the second covenant—viz., the sanctification of the soul.

A glance over these hastily sketched features will reveal the fact that all regenerated people are living under the first covenant, and although the covenant properly ended on the day of Pentecost, yet numbers of God's people insist upon its extension into the present time, and the strange fact confronts us that most of the Church of Christ are living to-day under the first covenant, which God has pronounced faulty; while the second covenant, with its superior nature and life, is before them untried and unentered, and has been thus before the Church for nearly two thousand years.

The Second Covenant.—This covenant began on the day of Pentecost, and is to terminate at the coming of the Son of God to judge the world. It was introduced with fire, and ends its work and history in presence of the fire of a burning world. It is, so to speak, walled in with fire. The new birth brings one into the first covenant, and baptism of the Holy Ghost and fire ushers us into the second covenant.

It is called a " new covenant.'' What happened at Pentecost was new. When the soul is sanctified it gets a new experience; it is not a former experience recovered.

It is a " better covenant." This is the language of Paul in Hebrews viii. 6. There is something better for the soul than regeneration. In sanctification, which is the second covenant, the promises are all better. The promise is not pardon, but *purity*. All filthiness shall be removed, all idols taken away, the heart shall be circumcised, the man shall be able to love God with all the heart. Any one can see that this is far ahead of the first covenant, and that this is the very promise made in sanctification.

The work is greater. God, in the second covenant, promises to " put his Spirit within us "—a promise confirmed by Christ in John xiv. 16, 17, in which appears the difference between the Spirit being with a man and in a man. Nor is this all. A deeper work is seen in the writing of God's law in the mind and heart; a deeper interior work; a permanent grace; the soul becomes a sanctuary, being part of the idea taught.

A greater knowledge is promised. "All shall know me, from the least to the greatest." It is remarkable how the blessing of sanctification qualifies the humblest, the youngest, and the least to be

teachers of the things of God. Instances rush to
the mind, one of which we mention occurring in
a certain State where a young man, although unable to read, yet was mighty in his knowledge of
spiritual things; so that the strange sight was witnessed of his sister reading the Bible to him while
he explained to her what it meant.

There is in the second covenant a deeper sense
of pardon. The frequent darkening and paralyzing remembrance of sins so well known to the regenerated man is taken away. "Their iniquities
will I remember no more." The soul has learned
the art of always looking to Christ instead of into
the guilty past, and hence the profounder sense of
peace and pardon.

There is a greater degree of spiritual life. Paul,
speaking of the first covenant, says that it "de-
cayeth," "waxeth old," and is "ready to vanish
away." This is the well-known experience of
many converted people. The life or blessing in
them constantly seems ready to perish or disappear. What prayers are required to retain it!
The second covenant ushers in a spiritual life
that does not wax old and does not depart at all,
but seems to grow fresher, brighter, and stronger
as the days and years go by. We are made to
marvel at the abundance and superabundance of

spiritual life that comes to the soul in holiness, or the second blessing. This constitutes one of the charms and peculiar glories of the experience. The soul is full and overflowing with life.

There is a greater privilege. " I will be to them a God." Here is taught especial protection and deliverance. God is seen by all to be on their side. God publicly owns them in ways unmistakable and convincing.

" And they shall be to me a people." Not simply people, but "*a* people." All Christians are God's people, but he can, by a distinguishing mark, make " a people " out of his people. They can become so devoted, so separate from sin and the world as to be known to all the world as God's peculiar people. And this is the very thing that is accomplished by the second covenant, or grace of sanctification. May this be the reader's consuming desire! It was that of the author; to be God's man, and to be recognized by everybody as God's man. So he sought with the whole heart the blessing that lies in the second covenant; and so, after living in the first for fourteen years, he entered at last by consecration, faith, and prayer into the second. The first was good, but in the language of inspiration he would testify to-day that the second is " better."

CHAPTER XIII.

ABRAHAM'S ALTAR.

THE remarkable scene in the fifteenth chapter of Genesis most curiously and yet correctly illustrates the way to obtain holiness.

The first step appears in the sixth verse, where it is plainly stated that Abraham was a justified man. This is the primary thing to consider in the case of one seeking holiness: Is he a child of God? It is absurd to think of becoming sanctified until justified.

The second step is God interviewing Abraham and promising him the land of Canaan. So the Lord continues to do to every regenerated man. The Canaan life—broad, plentiful, victorious, and restful—is held up invitingly to the soul. Like the man of God in the chapter, we ask how and whereby shall we know that we inherit it; and, like him, we recognize the coveted blessing as an inheritance.

The third step appearing in the narration is the bringing of whole offerings to God by Abraham. This he does by divine direction. There was a heifer, goat, ram, turtledove, and pigeon. In that peculiar presentation we read the words strength, appetite, usefulness, and virtue—all being brought to God in seeking a holy heart. Then it is noticeable that they were all whole offerings. The man of faith brought nothing piecemeal to God. All the strength, all the appetites, the whole undivided powers, and every virtue was laid on the altar. There is no escape from this divine requisition. The instant one says to God, " How shall I inherit the Canaan life? and how shall I know it?" the answer from heaven is, " Bring a whole offering to the altar." It is wonderful how some will bring the heifer of strength, and leave out the goat of the appetites; or bring the sheep of usefulness, and fail to bring the pigeon of swiftness for God, or the dove of a peaceful, unresisting life.

The fourth interesting feature that appears in the narrative is the strange things that happened to Abraham after his offerings were laid upon the altar.

First, the fowls came swooping down upon the carcasses. This is the invariable experience realized by the soul seeking sanctification. Instead of an instantaneous and delightful sense of acceptance, behold! the birds of night sweep down and try to destroy the consecration. Satan comes as a black bird of evil with beak and claws to tear the gift from the altar; doubts and fears circle around and settle upon these offerings made to heaven, and try to remove or destroy them. The sneers of the world, the remarks and ridicule of people in the Church, and members of the family, complete the flock of the dark-feathered tribe that at every consecration seem to rise up from the shades of the lower world and hover about, trying to alight with destructive bill and talons upon the soul's beautiful gift of itself to a holy God.

Second, "a deep sleep fell upon Abraham." This strange slumber or drowsiness of spirit comes to many. The person seeking holiness starts out with enthusiasm, fights for a while against difficulties, and then suddenly slackens effort, relaxes the ardent pursuit, and allows something like sleep to creep over the soul.

Third, a "horror of great darkness fell upon Abraham." This is a sadder experience. than that typified by the birds and the deep sleep. Very few seeking sanctification but have felt this horror. It amounts to a sudden despair as to their ever obtaining the blessing. The gloom at times is intense, and becomes a night of pitchy darkness upon the soul. Of course it is the work of the Evil One, whose untiring effort at this time is to get the gift from the altar, and failing in that he endeavors to fill the soul with such horrors of despair that the man himself will remove the offering. Satan knows that the altar sanctifies, and hence his active efforts through the birds and the horror of darkness to secure the removal of the gift from the dangerous place.

Many seekers of holiness suppose that the path will grow brighter with every step until the final purifying work is done. While this is the case with some, it is not so with the majority. Just as it is said to be darkest before dawn, and just as the reader will remember how full of shadows his heart was before his conversion, so oftentimes a horror of darkness gathers in the heart before the glorious eternal sunrise of Christ upon the soul in sanctification.

" The sun went down." This added to the heaviness of what had gone before. It certainly does look to the man seeking holiness that everything is against him. Such a person must remember that hell, the world, and a formal, backslidden Church are against him. But let him never forget that God is for him; that the suns of time may go down, but the Sun of Righteousness is ready to rise with healing in his wings. Let such an one also bear in mind that if the sun does go down the night makes a splendid background for the falling fire of heaven.

7

A fifth division of the narrative shows what Abraham did under these circumstances. What he did any one else can do, and must do if he would obtain the blessing of sanctification.

The chapter tells us he drove the birds away. Thank God, all of us can do that. Determine that neither devil nor man, fear nor doubt, shall pull from the altar what has been placed there for God alone. Fight the birds and drive them off. Refuse to let a doubt arise within the mind.

The author once saw a picture that held him with a strange power. It was a winter scene; the country was a wilderness and the land covered with snow. One tree stripped and bare stood spectrally in the background. A dead lamb lay upon the snow. On the limbs of the tree stood lines of black vultures, and around the lamb at a distance of twenty feet a heavy ring of the same sable ravens of death and carnage. Standing over the lamb protectingly was its mother. Her mouth was opened to send forth a bleat of distress. There was no sign of the shepherd. But so long as the sheep maintained her attitude of devotion and defense the hungry birds dared not approach. The lesson of the picture is, stand by the gift on the altar and keep off the birds. Wave them off with the hands of prayer and keep them back with the cries of supplication. The shepherd may not be in sight, but he is coming. Stand over your offering and protect it until Christ arrives.

Keep the sacrifice on the altar. If it slips or falls off, quietly put it back again. If it is removed a thousand times, restore it for the thousand and first time. The altar sanctifies the gift. All we need to do is to keep the gift on the altar.

Resist the disposition to fall asleep spiritually. Keep the soul aroused by a steady calling upon God. Throw off the feeling or temptation to despair; determine you will not despair.

Keep patient. A fretting spirit gets nothing, but defeats itself. Keep looking toward heaven. It is from that direction that the answer and the blessing and the fire must come. One can conceive of Abraham watching beside the altar, watching until the sun went down, and still watching and waiting for the fire after the sun had gone down. The light of the day had given place to the shadows of night, but there in the darkness was the same upturned face. So watches the soul for the descending flames of sanctification. It is the unchanging heavenward look that secures the blessing.

The sixth point in this wonderful chapter shows

what happened to Abraham from heaven. "Behold a smoking furnace." Here is the long-awaited fire. It came then to Abraham, came afterward to Moses, then to Isaiah, still later to the disciples, and will come even unto this day to all who will comply with the conditions laid down in this chapter. Let no soul be satisfied until it has obtained the baptism of fire.

But something else is seen beside the fire. The seventeenth verse adds a "burning lamp." The fire does the work and the lamp is let down to show what has been done. It stands most powerfully for the witness of the Spirit. It takes both fire and lamp to show up the entire work of the Holy Spirit in sanctification. The Holy Spirit falls in sanctifying power upon the soul, and throws light at the same moment to show what has been done. He works and witnesses at the same time. The fire and lamp go together; they "passed between those pieces." That is, the Holy Spirit permeates and passes through the strength and appetites, the virtues and the powers of the man, and separates and seals them all for God.

Finally comes a covenant by which God gives Abraham the whole land. It is yours "from the river of Egypt unto the great river." The sanctified man understands this. After the fire falls, the soul, for the first time, inherits the earth. It is an experience hard to describe, but not the less precious and blessed. The soul extracts a pleasure from nature and life never before known. It fairly exults in a sense of ownership of time, events, and the world itself. It draws a pleasure from the day and night, from the seasons—yes, from all things that the sinner knows nothing about and of which the regenerated man has only a faint idea. In a word, he owns everything from the rivers here on earth to the great river that flows out of the throne of God.

CHAPTER XIV.

THE EIGHT OFFERINGS.

IN the worship of the people of Israel there were a number of offerings. Each one represented some important truth or experience in the spiritual life. Most readers of the Bible have looked on them as disconnected acts of worship—each one complete in itself and having no relation to any other going before or coming after. The discovery that they are linked together and follow each other in an order agreeing exactly with the Christian experience has invested them with an additional and powerful charm to the author. The fact is that these blessings mentioned in the book of Leviticus record in a most impressive way the beginning, progress, and end of the Christian life on earth.

The Sin Offering.—This always stands for Christ. He is the lamb slain for our iniquity. Our one and only sin offering. It is vain to approach God in any other way. There is none other name under heaven whereby we can be saved.

The Burnt Offering.—The animal that consti-

(102)

tuted the burnt offering was slain and then consumed
to ashes either on the altar or "outside the gate."
Here we begin to see the worshiper; for while
Christ was, in a sense, consumed for us, we also
are to be consumed for him. When we speak of
things being burned the next thought suggested is
that of fire. After presenting Christ as our sin
offering the next thing to look for is fire, and
when we come to fire we come to holiness. After
making our sin offering we must press right on to
be burnt offerings. And how we will be burned!
The baptism of fire will burn up carnality or the
"old man" within us. Then the world and Satan
will endeavor to burn us up! How the devil loves
to build flaming fagots under and around the man
who has had the fire of God to fall upon his soul!
This fact accounts for the martyrs.

We should also burn ourselves up, so to speak,
for the glory of God. The life should be consumed for Christ. The writer saw on Dr. Adam
Clark's tomb, in London, carved on the stone
slab the figure of a candle expiring in its socket,
with the words underneath: "In giving light to
others I myself have been consumed." A glorious sentence. It is blessed to be a burnt offering
for God.

The Peace Offering.—This follows the other as

naturally as the light follows the sun. Peace comes
after being a burnt offering. The world seeks for
peace and happiness by flying from the fire and
every other form of pain and suffering. Men especially avoid the fiery baptisms of heaven. As
to how restless and miserable they all are, the
writer need not say. It is the man who loses his
life for Christ's sake that saves it! The burnt offering brings us to the peace offering. There will
be peace in the soul, and peace will come from all
such people to the world. There may be war at
first; for, as Christ said, he came to bring a sword.
The surgeon's knife precedes health. The man
baptized with fire, and now become God's burnt
offering, will create a stir. He has learned from
Christ how to plait a scourge and drive out wrong
things from the temple. But the end and glorious
accomplishment of all such lives is peace; peace to
the family, Church, and nations; a healthy and
abiding peace.

The Meat Offering.—This is what every Christian ought to be, and will be when fire-baptized.
A sanctified life is actual nourishment to the souls
of the people. Their words, prayers, conversation, spirit, and life are under the blessing of
Christ, like food to the heart. Who has not felt
this under the sermons of holy men? Madame

Guyon kept the soul of Fénelon from starving. "Feed my sheep," said the Saviour to Peter, and he did after the baptism of fire on the morning of the Pentecost. From that day he became a meat offering.

The Trespass Offering.—The author is very thankful that if a man should stumble and sin in the regenerated or sanctified life he is not undone. Some teach that he is, and throw souls into despair. God in thoughtful love has provided a remedy or way of recovery for the fallen one. Let the reader open the Bible and read about the trespass offering. If, says the Scripture, a man should be suddenly overtaken by a sin, let him bring at once a trespass offering to God. The truth taught is that while there is no plank in the platform of redemption that allows a man to sin, yet there is a plank that provides for his instantaneous recovery if he should sin. Take heart, ye stumbling, faltering ones; and if there is condemnation in the soul once more, then fly to God at once with the blood of Jesus. Offer your sin offering again as a trespass offering. He who forgave you for a lifetime of iniquity will certainly pardon you for one or a score of offenses.

The Thank Offering.—If a man has gone this far in the Christian life, he not only wants to be, but will be, a thank offering to God. Like the Jew, he will evince his gratitude to Heaven in a material and substantial way. But also with his lips will he praise God; while the life itself will be a glad, grateful, and constant consecration of its powers to God.

The Wave Offering.—This was made horizontally. It was, among other things, a public declaration of God, and spoke of a life abandoned to His will. So have we seen a flag waved from side to side. So every sanctified man tells God he can wave him and throw him about anywhere. The Lord waved the disciples all over the known world, and great was the result. He took Paul and made out of his willing life a wave offering that fluttered over Asia Minor, Greece, Italy, and Spain. He waved Wesley over Great Britain, Finney over New England, and Inskip over the United States. Who that reads these lines is willing to bow at this moment his head and heart and will, and whisper to Christ: "Lord Jesus, I am willing to be a wave offering for thee?"

The Heave Offering.—This was presented to God with a vertical motion. The whole sanctified life should be a heave offering. We should cast everything into heaven: hopes, joys, prayers, ambitions, treasures, and ourselves. The author has seen just such men, who stood on earth and pitched everything they could lay hold of into heaven. Judge McGehee, of Mississippi, kept heaving his money upward to God. Charles G. Finney kept heaving souls into glory.

Finally, at death the man himself becomes a heave offering. He spent his days in throwing blessed things into heaven, and one day he lost his balance and went upward himself into glory. Enoch, after walking with God a long time, suddenly became a heave offering. How the people missed him! Elijah was a wave offering over Israel and Judah, but one morning on a mountain side beyond Jordan he suddenly left Elisha's side and went upward to dwell with God forever. He had become a heave offering.

John S. Inskip became a burnt offering in Brooklyn with the words on his lips: "I am, O Lord, wholly and forever thine." He was next a wave offering for God all over the United States for twenty years; and then at Ocean Grove on his deathbed, while waving a palmetto fan and whispering "Victory," he became a heave offering.

The course is ended, the last offering is rendered, and the offerers vanish one by one into the heavens. With the last gift they are gone, and we are left behind crying as did Elisha: "My father, my father, the chariot of Israel, and the horsemen thereof.''

So one day we will come to a like hour. It will be a like hour indeed if we have rendered to God all the offerings laid down in this chapter. May the words of the following stanza describe what shall occur to the writer, and to the reader of these lines, when the soul leaves the body:

> Or if on joyful wing
>   Cleaving the sky,
> Sun, moon, and stars forgot,
>   Upward I fly;
> Still all my song shall be,
> Nearer my God to thee,
>   Nearer to thee.

CHAPTER XV.

THE ark stands for the human heart or soul. The things in the ark represent those heavenly deposits or works of grace which God would make the property and possession of the soul.

One thing noticeable was the two tables of commandments. This corresponds to the promise made to write his laws and statutes in our minds and hearts. Another thing was the manna, which always typified Christ, the true bread sent down from heaven. The manna abiding in the ark symbolized the indwelling of Christ in the soul; which blessing takes place according to promise in sanctification. The third article was the rod that bloomed, budded, and bore almonds. Remaining always in this state, it signified that constant fruitfulness of soul and life that is certain to follow the sanctifying grace of God. The ark with its treasures is plainly made to typify a holy heart. Hence the chapter showing David going forth to obtain the ark and bring it in to Jerusalem is a powerful symbolic teaching of a man seeking holiness.

In this going forth for the ark, the vicissitudes by the way, and its final entry with David into Zion some very striking lessons are given. These lessons are found in the consideration of the characters that appear in the sixth chapter of Second Samuel, and the parts they bore to the ark. What transpires here happens at the present day. David appears and reappears in the midst of other people who in various ways affect him in a manner most significant. Our space admits of only a brief mention of each as they come up, making as they appear that history of the holiness movement seen in many places to-day.

David the Seeker.—He goes out with chosen men. Not any and all seek and get the ark of a holy heart. Every Church shows a band of chosen ones who seek heart purity. These may not be choice ones in the sight of man, but nevertheless are divinely approved. David places the ark on " a new cart." It is vain to look for the blessing of holiness in an unregenerated state. We must have a new heart first, and in that God will place the ark of his covenant. As David proceeded with the ark they all played before the Lord on all manner of musical instruments, and were very glad. The possesssion of a holy heart starts the singing in the soul that Paul speaks of;

that gladness and joy that Isaiah speaks of as filling the sanctified as they go on their happy way to Zion. Holiness is so joy-inspiring that the writer never knew a man that began seeking it but felt at once the rise of the spiritual thermometer into higher altitudes of gladness. Often the speech is made: "I never enjoyed religion more than when I was seeking this blessing." Musical instruments form a most appropriate setting for the ark.

Uzzah.—Here is a man about whom we know little save that "he put forth his hand to the ark of God, and took hold of it." People are still repeating this offense. Some are doing it patronizingly. They would take the cause of holiness under their wings. They have not the blessing, but they will protect and defend and steady the ark. They act as if the cause of God was a sickly something that needed nursing, instead of being, as it is, omnipotence accommodating its pace to the step of an animalcule! O the absurdity of human patronage! A gnat trying to shelter an archangel under its wing is a piece of wisdom compared to it. Others touch the ark authoritatively. They would repress it here and stop it yonder. They act as if they owned the ark and its march through earth depended on them. They send word from various seats and positions in the Church that the ark must not be allowed entrance here or there or yonder; that such a man coming with the ark must be rebuked and stopped. In various ways they lay their hand upon the great holiness movement of God. Still others touch the ark hurtfully. They try in various ways to injure and to affect its progress. Preachers are silenced and removed from their charges who are seen marching with and at the head of the ark. Members of the Church are ostracized socially, and excommunicated ecclesiastically, for being in the procession, singing and praising the beauty of holiness. Ridicule flows from pen and tongue, while the heavy hand of Church power falls upon the ark that is being brought up with such gladness to Zion.

The Bible says "the anger of the Lord was kindled against Uzzah, and God smote him there for his error; and there he died by the ark of God." The penalty of laying the hand improperly upon the doctrine, experience, and cause of holiness is death. Dr. Finney, the evangelist, tells of a preacher who greatly resisted a revival of holiness in a certain town, and one morning was found dead in his bed. The penalty for laying hands on the ark is death—not always a physical, but invariably spiritual death. A well-known, prominent minister told the writer that in a certain State he had known an attack on holiness to be made by preachers who had been useful and successful before, but after that they never had another conversion. The writer has seen many die spiritually for the way they treated the ark. He has seen not only individuals, but Churches, wither under the judgment of an offended God. Not always was it an instantaneous spiritual death, but gradual, such as took place with the fig tree that Christ cursed and such as came upon Jerusalem when Christ stood before it and pronounced it desolate. While he uttered the words "your house is left unto you desolate," birds sang on, the sun was shining, the palaces gleaming, the inhabitants going on absorbed in business and pleasure as usual. And long after the sharpest eye could see no difference. The city gleamed on the hill side, the smoke of incense and sacrifice still ascended, the sound of song and laughter still rang out in house and street, chariots and horses were coming and going as usual; and yet the decay had started from the moment that Christ had said "desolate," and finally culminated in a national death that has solemnized the whole observant world.

So, gradually has the writer seen a Church de-

8

cay and die that has smitten the ark, and so has he seen the individuals who denied and decried and resisted the doctrine of holiness begin to fade as a leaf, until finally there fell from their own lips the confession that they had lost every particle of the light of their justification.   They die gradually, but not the less certainly; for it is God that smites, and his blows are unerring.   They die before the ark of the Lord.   The ark lives, but they die.

David the Discouraged.—David became afraid and discouraged at this time.   The Scripture says he would not bring the ark up, but carried it aside and allowed another man to take possession.   This is a spectacle we frequently behold.   Men grow discouraged and fall away from holiness as they take note of its demands and solemn retributions. They give up seeking the blessing.   They carry it aside, relegate it to a lower plane, act as if it was not so important after all, and let some one else obtain the blessing.

Obed-edom.—He was a man who received the ark into his house when other men were afraid of it and were disposed to let it alone.   Obed-edom is not alone.   His spiritual posterity is increasing all over the land.   There are many in the lowly places of this world who gladly open heart and house for the blessing of heart purity or full salvation which does not seem so popular with those in higher walks. They gladly take up what others neglect or reject, and enthrone in life and home what others are willing, for various reasons, to set aside.

So when the ark of holiness appeared in a certain large city the leading members of the Church refused to accept it and permitted it to be turned aside, while the writer and a few others gladly received it. And when the ark appeared in another leading city and was offered to the congregations it was rejected by most of them, and the doors of a single church were opened to receive it; so the ark turned aside and rested in a place that should have been called "Obed-edom" from that day. The eleventh verse says that God "blessed Obed-edom, and all his household." Of course he did, and will do so, and does do so in these very days. The Church or individual that does not fight it, but receives the blessing of holiness, will always be blessed.

David Seeks Again and Succeeds.—What was it that caused the king to come again after the ark? The twelfth verse informs us: "And it was told King David, saying, The Lord hath blessed the house of Obed-edom, and all that pertaineth unto him, because of the ark of God." In other words, he saw what a mistake he had made and how much he had lost by his former conduct, and now determined to rectify his error and regain what he had lost. He went once more for the ark, and this time brought it up. Truly if anything will cause the neglecters and rejectors of holiness to change their views and seek the despised grace, it will be the good tidings and sight of those whom God is blessing.

That God does and is blessing them is seen in the shining face, joyful life, and abundant labors of the individual, and the marvelous prosperity of the Church which flings its doors open to shelter the doctrine and obtain the experience of perfect love. Such spectacles are calculated to bow the hearts of men like David, and they will say: " This is of God, and it is for me as well as for them; I will arise and seek and obtain it, with the help and favor of Heaven."

In the twelfth, fourteenth, and fifteenth verses we read that when David had secured the ark and was moving onward to Jerusalem he was full of "gladness," and "danced" and "shouted." All this accords with the sanctified experience. For real gladness, for uplift of spirit, and frequent uplifts of body; for real, genuine shouting, commend me to the man who has the second blessing. The shouting machine is placed within us when the heart is purified. It is impossible to successfully imitate it. Regenerated people look on its constant working with wonder and sometimes skepticism, but their doubt does not interrupt its heavenly operations, while, at the same time, they rarely make an effort to compete with it by anything of similar character of their own invention. The writer once saw an unsanctified man try it, and it was a doleful and evident failure. He ran by the way of the plain and outran Cushi, but had really no message to deliver. He assayed as the magicians tried to imitate Moses, but his machine did not work. It had a rusty, grating sound. The wheels ran heavily. So the brother soon stopped and sunk into a silence that lasted all the rest of the protracted meeting. The writer once said to a body of Christians who doubted the rejoicing and shouting of a sanctified band that if they thought such a spirit could be worked up they were at liberty to prove the fact against us, and that we would retire and leave them in the room, with closed doors and windows, to work up the enthusiasm and put in motion their shouting machines. They did not accept the challenge, and there was in their eyes an unmistakable expression of conviction that they could not, by any human might, reproduce the gladness and exhilaration of the pentecostal scene going on before them. The shouting grace comes with holiness.

Michal, the Unfriendly Observer and Despiser.
—The wife of David stood looking through the windows at her husband as he sung, leaped, and shouted his way along at the head of the ark. What a cold-blooded picture she made! "And she despised him in her heart."   Many times have we beheld scenes exactly similar. Night after night, around the church altar where Davids were rejoicing and shouting over the presence of the ark of holiness in the camp, has the writer seen people sitting back in their pews and gazing through their eyeglasses and spectacles like Michal did through the window. The heart sickened at the sight as we said: " How is it that a being can thus look unmoved on the work of God and upon the holy rapture of a soul that has abandoned itself to His holy will?"   Their gazing was as cold-blooded as that of Michal, and declared the fact of the same untouched heart and Spirit-forsaken soul. They despised the whole movement and its leaders in their hearts.

But let us be patient. They do not see as they should. They fail to understand what they do see. They have had Sauls for fathers; and so let us commend them to God, and—shout on.

David's Life.—How did David act under this peculiar trial? He must have seen the scornful face at the window. It is delightful to see how strong he had become. The ark was not forsaken this time, but he goes on steadily from grace to glory. Some people would have given up right here because the wife or husband, preacher or friend wore a skeptical smile. The seventeenth, eighteenth, nineteenth, and twentieth verses tell us that David went straight on to the tabernacle, offered burnt offerings, peace offerings, blessed the people, gave them bread, flesh, and wine, and then returned to bless his household. This is the way to do, and is the way that many are doing. If any person is going to bless the people, it is the sanctified man. The common salutation with him is: "God bless you." If any person is giving spiritual bread and meat to the congregation, it is he. And as for the wine of salvation, which cheers and warms the heart, fills the mouth with songs, shouts, and holy laughter, and reproduces Pentecost, he is the one above all others who knows best how to bring it down from the skies and pour it out for the people.

Michal, the Ridiculer and Opposer.—The wife

of David is not satisfied with an inward feeling of
contempt, but meets the rejoicing monarch and
says, with stinging words and scornful manner:
"How glorious was the King of Israel to-day,
who uncovered himself to-day in the eyes of the
handmaids of his servants, as one of the vain fel-
lows shamelessly uncovereth himself!"

The ridicule and opposition came right in the
midst of David's joy and good deeds. And it
does so still.   Let the sanctified soul look for ridicule and obstacles of this kind at any time, and be
astonished if they do not come.   Especially in moments of highest joy and usefulness will Michal
stand before you with scornful eyes and words
overflowing with bitterness and sarcasm.   The
judgment that came upon Michal for her conduct
was barrenness.   The twenty-third verse says:
"Therefore Michal the daughter of Saul had no
child unto the day of her death."   One of the
noteworthy facts about the ridiculers, scoffers,
and opposers is their entrance upon a life of spiritual barrenness.   Their ministry and labors become unfruitful.   They preach and work in the
Church, but souls are no longer born unto God
through their efforts as of yore.   The judgment
of barrenness, for mocking at the presence,
work, and power of the Holy Ghost falls upon

them. They bear no more children unto God unto the day of their death.

Fifth and Last View of David.—Will he go down under this new assault? A man's foes are they of his own household. Spiritual corpses are in every home of the land, slain by the household foe. "The hand that betrayed me is with me on the table." It takes more grace to withstand the opposition at home than the attacks on us from without. The home foe is always present. The home circle is the hardest to be convinced. "Neither did his brethren believe on him."

How will David deport himself now? He that grew discouraged in the beginning, will he not lose heart now, and say there is no use in a man trying to be religious and devoted with an unbelieving wife on his hands to mock and oppose him? Far from it: he stands erect, noble in speech and manner before the home mocker. He never appeared to better advantage or was more to be admired by earth and heaven than at this moment. He showed greater courage than when he met the bear, attacked the lion, and slew Goliath. Listen to the unutterably beautiful and brave words of the man. Take them sentence by sentence:

"*It was before the Lord.*" That means that the action which excited criticism was not gone

through with to attract the attention of man: the
waving hand, the uplifted face, the leaping body,
all sprang from an absorbed contemplation and
enjoyment of God.   How these actions affected
the judgments of men did not enter the mind.   It
was before the Lord.

"*And I will yet be more vile than this.*"
Thank God for the determination to go farther
and deeper in the life of Christian humility, no
matter who mocks.   Some people, when they hear
the jeers and laughter at their expense, say, " I
will be less vile;" and begin to trim and alter in the
impossible task of trying to please a gainsaying
and hypocritical world.   John the Baptist came in
one way, the Son of man in another; and neither
one pleased the captious nation.   " If I pleased
men, I should not be the servant of Christ," said
Paul.   Let us not try to please the world, but to
its mocking, reply in the spirit of Christ: " I will
yet be more vile."

"*And will be base in mine own sight.*"   Here
the man of God struck the bottom.   No depth be-
neath this.   Few get here.   Few want to be base
in their own sight.   The natural heart prefers exaltation, praise, honorable places, and public mention.   The band of people is small who are willing
to be nothing before men that Christ may be all

and everything. When a man is willing to sink out of sight or appear base and obscure in God's work he is living very near the throne; but while ripe for glory, was never more powerful for God's service.

Paul started out with saying that he was not one whit behind the chiefest of the apostles. But in a better spirit he wrote that he was the " least of the apostles." A few years later he wrote again, saying that " he was less than the least of the saints." Still later he pens the words that he was the chief of sinners. Not that he was a sinner then, but he was speaking of what he once was, and how he would be still but for the saving and transforming grace of Christ.

How lonely we get as we go deeper in the divine life. Michal could not understand the speech or appreciate the spirit of her husband; but he never was a grander man, and never appeared nobler to Heaven, than when he said to the gainsaying partner of his life who had utterly failed to see the religious beauty of his life: " It was before the Lord, and I will yet be more vile than this and will be base in my own sight, if necessary for the glory of God."

CHAPTER XVI.

THE two cleansings of the temple by the Saviour constitutes another powerful symbolic proof of two works of grace in the soul. A number of interesting discoveries are made by a little study of the scenes as described in the word.

The first fact we notice is that many people at first see only one cleansing of the temple. They suppose that the evangelists all wrote of the same occurrence, when the truth is that there were two distinct purifications of the sanctuary and separated by an interval of time of fully three years. So at first the majority of people believe there is but one cleansing of the soul. They read of spiritual birth and baptism, regeneration and sanctification, and suppose that they refer to one and the same thing. Later on some of them discover that there are two works, distinct as operations of grace and clearly separated by time.

A second fact of interest is that many who see that there are two cleansings of the temple mentioned in the gospel yet believe they were works of an identical nature, the second being simply a

(124)

repetition or going over again of the first. But here again prayerful study is rewarded by the discovery that the two purifications were strikingly different, and this very difference constitutes the strength of the argument in this chapter. While there is a similarity, the points of dissimilarity are so great that the thoughtful and spiritual mind must be impressed and magnify the great God who stamps the truths of his salvation in such a powerful way in symbolism. When discovered by the writer he was thrilled at this divine confirmation in type of what is elsewhere taught so positively in doctrine and commandment.

It is curious how, in the same way just mentioned, men who must admit that the words " regeneration " and " sanctification " are not synonymous yet insist that they mean the same thing; that sanctification is a repetition of regeneration, a deeper going over of the first work, and a ripening or mellowing, so to speak, of the original fruit. So many of us believed once, until through prayer and illumination of our minds by the Spirit we saw what is so plainly taught in the two cleansings of the temple: that there are two blessings or works of grace for the soul.

Let us notice the difference between the first and the second purifications of the sanctuary as taught in the gospel. True, we grant they look alike. As Christ is seen in both instances overturning the tables of the money changers and driving out the cattle that lined the courts, we are not surprised that some would say that it was a repeating of the first work. So there is a marked similarity between conversion and the blessing of holiness. At the new birth Christ overturned and cast out many things. But one strange fact about the heart in which inbred sin is left is its peculiar aptness to return to things formerly surrendered to or cast out by the Saviour. The man gives up tobacco and goes back to it, he abjures the animal and yields again to it, he promises onetenth of his income to God and is faithful for a while and forgets or neglects the duty. The tables are again set up, the cattle of questionable practices are again seen in the courts of the Lord's temple. So when the sanctifying grace of God comes: over go the tables again, the animals are now driven out for good, and the vows, duties, and sacrifices undertaken but not faithfully adhered to are again resumed, and this time forever.

But after this we notice the difference.

First, in the second cleansing, Christ came as a King. In the first purification he was unknown.

Before the people were aware this mysterious One whom few knew was standing looking around upon the desecrated courts of his Father, and then quickly began casting out that which was sinful and forbidden. But at the second entry he came in as a King. "Fear not, daughter of Sion, behold, thy King cometh." This prophecy related to the second entry into the temple. Sanctification is the second entry of Christ into the soul. The first time he was little known, but this time he enters as its crowned and welcomed King and Ruler. The whole life from that time on is one of perfect subjection and obedience to him.

Second, he came deliberately. Malachi, writing about it, said: "The Lord, whom ye seek, shall suddenly come to his temple." Before the people knew it Christ stood as an unknown Prophet and Reformer in their midst doing his cleansing work. But here in his second entry his approach is heralded, and his presence momentarily expected. This strikingly shows the difference between the obtainment of pardon and holiness. In a swift hour many are converted, and find Christ in the heart casting out and cleansing. But in sanctification the work is one of deliberation. The man prepares for Christ. Days are spent in looking for him and awaiting his glorious and royal incoming.

This same contrast between suddenness and deliberateness is seen in the unexpected finding of the treasure by the wayfarer and the calm search for the pearl of great price given by the merchantman; the rapid crossing of the Red Sea by the children of Israel fleeing from Egyptian bondage, and their quieter preparation to cross the Jordan into the Canaan of rest and plenty. All three scenes teach the same fact.·

Third, he entered with symbols of humility. He came as a King, yet riding upon an ass. A profound meekness and humbleness of spirit is the attendant and result of sanctification. Men suppose the testifying to a clean heart betrays spiritual egotism and pride, but the soul is never humbler than when made pure. The war charger and what it stands for, the pomp, parade, and earthly trappings that men so emphasize are discounted and set aside; while the lowly method and despised instrumentality are used in meekness of spirit and with full trust in God.

Fourth, He entered with the rejoicing and shouting of the multitude. There is no doubt but that sanctification loosens the tongue and inaugurates the " joy experience " of the soul. The kingdom of God is righteousness, peace, and joy in the Holy Ghost. Many live in the first two counties, but fail to cross the border into a spiritual district "where the flowers bloom forever and the sun is always bright." The words "hosannah" and "hallelujah" are heard suspiciously and coldly by the majority of Christians to-day. They are only approved as found in the Bible or in the biography of some good man who has been dead fifty years. But when they leap joyously and spontaneously to the lip, as they do with sanctified people, they and their utterers are an offense to the modern Church. Whoever receives Christ the second time may prepare for a life of rejoicing and praise. He brings it with him when he comes.

Fifth, Christ entered with the clothing of the people under his and their feet. The Scripture says they strewed their garments in the way. Nothing of the kind was seen in the first entry. The thought suggested to the mind by this is that it takes sanctification to place the dress question where it belongs. A man truly gets the garment business under his feet when he gets sanctified. Besides this, we observe that many a garment comes off and goes down when Christ comes into the life as King. Very little change is noticed in one's attire on the first entry, but after the second cleansing the revolution and reformation is marked.

Sixth, he entered with palm branches. The

9

palm is a symbol of victory, and when the heart receives sanctification victory begins from that hour;
victory over temptation, doubt, sin, and Satan.
And it is a constant victory. The regenerated
life, as usually lived, might be characterized by
the weeping willow. The ordinary Christian experience is one of tears, sighs, stumblings, and
frequent hangings of the harp upon the willow.
There is generally a deploring over inward cor-
ruptions and a proneness to leave God. They lament that their course is a zigzag and an "up and
down" course. They confess to many crooked
steps; and in the class meeting experience their favorite resort and flight, after such humbling confes-
sions, is to the graveyard with pathetic mention of
those "who have gone before." The willow is
their tree. They prefer its drooping attitude and
mournful sighs. But the instant the man gets
sanctified he leaves the graveyard, cuts down the
willow, grasps his harp in one hand and swing-
ing his palm branch in the other, goes on his way
with shouting, rejoicings, and hosannahs toward
the kingdom of glory. The mournful experience
is ended, he lets the dead alone; and full of the
sweet gladness of a full and constant salvation he
waves his palm branch and presses on his tri-

umphant way, through toil, duty and difficulty, to heaven.

Seventh, Christ entered with certain classes of people. They were poor people, women and children; the very classes that are looked down on with contempt in the spiritual life by an arrogant world. When Jesus enters the soul in sanctifying power he brings in the despised companies of earth. He creates a peculiar love for the poor. Sanctification is a wonderful leveler of human distinctions. It doesn't stop to notice the difference between silk and calico, jeans and broadcloth, but prizes people for the sake of their immortal souls. Hence there is no partiality—no saying to a rich man "Come up here," and to the poor man " Sit down there under my footstool." A marvelous work has been done that delivers the soul from a grievous bondage imposed upon it by the hand of wealth and custom. As for the women, who are their warmest advocates to-day but sanctified men of God? We recognize their equality in every respect, and bid them come up and fill every station and discharge every work for which God has filled them and the Holy Ghost calls them. In no assembly is a woman guaranteed more liberty than in a holiness meeting. Christ, in the second entry, brings her in with all her rights and wrongs, her gifts and privileges. As for the children, they become the recipients of a new and tenderer interest and consideration than was known before.

Eighth, when Christ entered, the blind and lame were brought to him and were healed. It is astonishing what works of grace follow sanctification. One person receiving the blessing means a number brought at once to know the pardon of God; and if the doctrine is preached and received in a Church (not fought), the result invariably is scores and hundreds of conversions. The blind receive their sight, the lame are healed, the spiritually dead are raised. In the Church in which the author was pastor, and where Christ was allowed to enter the second time in sanctifying power, for the two years he remained there was scarcely a week that a number of people were not saved at the altar.

Ninth, the chief priests and scribes beheld this second entry and cleansing with the results mentioned in this chapter, and were much displeased.

Is it not marvelous that they should feel offended and object to Christ's exaltation, the spontaneous joy of the people, the Heaven-inspired praises of the multitude, and the healing of the afflicted who pressed about him? And yet they did; and God's

Word makes the statement. They were offended at every feature of the triumphal procession, but especially at the shouts, praises, and religious demonstrations. They requested the Saviour to quiet the multitude. His reply was that if they ceased the stones would cry out.

The chief priests and doctors are still offended at the glorious second entry and cleansing work of Christ in the soul and in the Church. It does seem that they would rejoice over the exalting doctrine of the power of Christ's blood to purify, and be glad to listen to the spontaneous praises of his people and to see the souls of men brought into light, life, peace, and purity, while Christians rejoice and shout as they are filled with the Holy Ghost. Not so, and alas for it! there are many in high places in the Church who are " much displeased" at the whole thing. The stripping of garments; the waving of palm branches; the leveling of class distinctions; the noise of rapturous singing and shouting; the leaping of the restored lame man; the thrilling cry of the healed, the pardoned, and the purified in the temple; the words " hosannah " and " hallelujah " on many lips; the life, movement, and seeming confusion of pentecostal scenes—all meet with their unqualified displeasure and open condemnation. Many of the chief

priests, scribes, and doctors in the Church to-day
are " much displeased " and manifest their displeasure unmistakably.   So history repeats itself,
and here in the nineteenth century we are called
upon to witness and pass through scenes of identical character with that which took place on that
wonderful morning in the city of Jerusalem nearly
two thousand years ago.

CHAPTER XVII.

THE TWO RESTS.

SUCH is the slowness of the mind to grasp spiritual things that thousands read the following passage in Matthew hundreds of times before noticing that it speaks of two rests for the soul: "Come unto me, all ye that labor and are heavy laden, and I will give you rest. Take my yoke upon you, and learn of me; for I am meek and lowly in heart: and ye shall find rest unto your souls. For my yoke is easy, and my burden is light." The reader notices that the word "rest" occurs twice, but hastily supposes it to be a mere repetition; that the same fact or blessing is twice stated. A closer scrutiny reveals the mistake. There are two rests in the spiritual life, obtained in different ways and at different times.

The First Rest.—This rest is offered to the unconverted. The expression "all ye that labor and are heavy laden" evidently refers to the sinner. The word "come" unmistakably teaches the fact of moral distance.

This first rest is given. "Come unto me, . . . and I will give you rest." This is what is expe-

rienced by the repenting and believing soul in its
first interview and communion with Christ.   Rest
has been freely given.

The first rest is obtained by coming to Christ.
This is the condition laid down in the passage, and
is the very condition of receiving pardon.   Nothing is exacted of the penitent sinner but to come
to Christ.   There is not a word about consecration or duties taken up, but the simple invitation
" come."

The Second Rest.—This blessing appears in the
twenty-ninth verse, and is what Mr. Wesley calls
the " second blessing " and what his brother
Charles termed in his hymns the " second rest."

> Let us all in Thee inherit,
> Let us find that second rest.

This is the same rest that Paul speaks so much
about in the fourth and fifth chapters of Hebrews.
About it we notice, as taught in the word of Matthew, several very interesting things that completely differentiate it from the rest mentioned in
the preceding verse.   It is not the rest of heaven
as we once thought it meant, but a soul rest that
the Christian is privileged to receive as a second
blessing.   It is promised to Christians.   The language teaches that the recipients of this blessing
have been with Christ and have engaged in his

service before receiving the grace. The same people were addressed, but they are told of two blessings that come at very different times and under very different circumstances. It is not those that labor and are heavy laden that are promised the second rest, but those that bear Christ's yoke and have taken him as their teacher.

This second rest is found; the first was given. The two cannot possibly be made to agree. A gift is one thing; something found is another. The passage teaches that while people are in the service of God the second rest is suddenly realized or found. This is the teaching of the Bible, and harmonizes with the experience of a vast number who in this age and in other centuries have received the second rest or blessing. They obtained it while in the service of God. While walking in the light as he is in the light they found themselves, in a moment, cleansed from all sin; suddenly, while keeping his word, the love of God was perfected within them. They found the second rest in the Christian life.

It is obtained by consecration and faith. Christ makes the way to the blessing clear. " Take my yoke upon you." The yoke stands for his doctrines—for all of them—and for the most unpopular of them as well. It stands for his service—for a complete surrender to his will and work. No figure or symbol scarcely could be stronger to convey the idea of a complete and irrevocable consecration than that of the yoke. When the ox has it placed upon his neck, the bow slipped into the hole, and the key put in place, he is then fastened. He is, so to speak, a fixture. In just such a way the man seeking sanctification must accept the yoke, bow, and key, and be finally and forever given up and over to God. Like the love slave nailed to the door, he is pinned to Christ's yoke or nailed to the cross, just as you please. He can no more go here or there as it may please him. There is no more going ahead or lagging behind or wandering out on the side of the road according to vagaries of mind and heart, but he is fastened to the symbol wagon. He bears the yoke as the Lord once bore the cross. He is the Lord's man from this time.

A second thing to do Christ adds in the words " learn of me."   Here is humility, docility, obedience, and faith all taught in one sentence. " Learn of me."   Would that all doubters of sanctification would go to Christ instead of one another for information ! How soon they would rejoice in soul rest ! " Learn of me," he said. Don't go to men, don't take the *dictum* of preachers. Surely the man who denies the experience can know nothing about it. A preacher went to another who outranked him officially, and desired to know whether there was a second blessing or work of grace. He received a negative answer and gave up the search. He should have gone to Christ instead of man, and then he would to-day be rejoicing in the second rest instead of being its ridiculer and condemner. If we go to Christ, sit at his feet, and learn of him, we will soon find that he is able, willing, and ready to make the soul pure and let it find a heaven on earth in its entrance upon and enjoyment of the second rest.

The same passage in Matthew tells what happens after the gracious obtainment. The yoke becomes easy. It is not so to the regenerated. There is much chafing and fretting in the Christian life. The doctrines hurt, the service galls, and so there is fretfulness and complaint. Christ has a blessing that makes the yoke delightful to bear. The blessing of holiness fits the yoke, and adjusts it so perfectly to the soul that there is no chafing and galling, and hence no complaining. Sanctification is religion made easy. It becomes a joy and luxury to serve Christ. The yoke is transformed into a wing.

The " burden is light." That is, anything that

Christ places upon you, or allows to come upon you, is light. There was a time, before the reception of the blessing of holiness, when every burden that came in the Christian life was heart-depressing and paralyzing. But after entering into the second rest the burdens that saddened and bore the soul down to the earth became feather weights. The ridicule, opposition, and persecution of the world you can throw upon your shoulders, as did Samson the brazen gates of Gaza, and bear them away to a certain gray hill called Calvary, and there leave them with praises of tongue and rejoicings of spirit. Christ's burden, all that he places upon you, or allows the Church or world to cast upon you, shall in the " second rest " become light.

And now notice the third result: "And ye shall find rest unto your souls." What a blessed sentence this is! What a life of spiritual calm and heart rest it describes! " Rest unto your souls." Rest away down in your soul, all through the soul, and all the time in the soul. Repose is seen in the manner, serenity in the face, and an unfathomable rest gathers and settles in the eyes. The man was never busier for Christ, but goes to his work and returns from it with this inward rest always abiding in the heart. He found it under the yoke and while learning at the feet of Christ.

CHAPTER XVIII.

IT was a long time before the writer discovered there were two fluids to be quaffed in the kingdom of grace. Both are made to appear at the marriage in Cana of Galilee. It is marvelous how slowly the mind makes spiritual discoveries. Men have all along seen and must still see a difference in the religious experience of Christians and which is not to be accounted for by education or temperament. A calm, unprejudiced investigation will reveal the fact that the dissimilarity springs not from varying natures and dispositions, but from the possession and enjoyment of two distinct blessings or operations of divine grace. One may be called the water and the other the wine of salvation. One refreshes; the other exhilarates. The water of regeneration is grateful, renewing, and reviving to the heart; while the wine of sanctification fires the soul, intoxicates the spirit, and fills the lips with rapturous songs and holy, happy laughter.

It is a wonderful day in the religious life when a man has the contents of his cup changed from

(141)

water to wine. The world stands amazed, and one part of the Church is often scandalized and another part skeptical and explanatory of the phenomenon; but the man himself, drinking in the rich, red wine of salvation, is not mystified or skeptical himself, and praises God with shoutings and singing as he drinks on and drinks deeper of the blessed liquid made in heaven and that is sent down not to befog the mind and deplete the power of man, but to cheer his heart, warm his soul, exalt his spirit, and uplift the whole life in a transport of joy to God.

The disciples drank of the water of regeneration for over three years, but on the morning of Pentecost God sent them wine in the form of the blessing of sanctification. What a time they had that morning! The city was moved at the sight, and insisted that they were drunk. It was true, but not on the liquors of the earth, but with the wine made in the New Jerusalem.

The writer drank water for fourteen years in the Christian life; but four years ago, learning that he could have wine, he sought and obtained it in the second blessing, and drinks it now exclusively. To many of his friends he appears partially intoxicated and unaccountably excited, but the explanation is found in the change of fluids. He is well satisfied with the change that keeps his heart aglow, his soul full of singing, and his heart and lips overflowing with thanksgiving and praises to God.

Now and then we meet with a sanctified man who drinks deeper than others of this new and strong wine. Not long since we saw one at an Annual Conference. It was impossible to look on his glowing face and hear his mingled shouts and laughter without being melted and stirred. It was an eye-filling, soul-warming, and infectious sight. The man was drunk with religion. Lord increase the tribe! It was just such a spectacle that convicted the city of Jerusalem. And whenever the scene is repeated cities will be moved and convicted again. Certainly if there is anything that can and will awe the world, it is the spectacle of men drunk on an invisible wine, poured out by unseen hands, and evidently sent from another world. Think of it! Men drunk on religion! The Church intoxicated with the grace and love and glory of God! When shall we see this day? Who wonders that three thousand souls were saved at such a time in the city of Jerusalem? Such a sight surpasses in power all volumes of Christian evidence. This is Christ himself made evident. The eternal world with its forces wheels before the sight of the soul, and men are awed, heart-pricked, convinced, and cry out: " What must we do to be saved?"

When will the Church quit sipping water and go to drinking the wine of the Spirit? The ruler of the feast said to the bridegroom: "Thou hast kept the good wine until now." What they had at the beginning was fair, but the best was given at the last. All say the same who receive the blessing of sanctification. We address the Bridegroom, the Lord Jesus, and utter like words: " Surely thou hast kept the best until now."

How shall we obtain the wine? There are two things to do. This is what is told every seeker after sanctification. We find it taught in numerous places and in different ways throughout the Scripture. The same teaching appears in the scene at Cana of Galilee.

One thing to do is to " fill the water pots with water up to the brim." Here is the perfect consecration that is demanded of the soul that seeks purity. The measure that Christ requires must be given. All that he demands must be met. The water pots must be filled, and filled *up to the brim.* The merchantman seeking the pearl " sold all he had " to get it. The young man aroused for a moment with desires to be like Christ was told that he must " sell all." Right here is the trouble

with many. They hate to feel utterly emptied;
they would like to reserve a few coins to meet to-
morrow's demands; they would like to defend
themselves against their detractors just once more;
they would like to bid farewell to the friends at
home, and have one more evening at the old farm-
house. The word is: " Forsake all and follow
me." And the same command is projected here
in illustrative form: " Fill the water pots with water up to the brim." Let the consecration be so
complete that not another drop is needed, nor remains to be given. How well the soul knows
when this is done! How conscious it is of its own
integrity, obedience, and abandon to God! When
" up to the brim " the thrilled soul sings to itself
and to God:

> My all to Christ I've given,
> My talents, time, and voice,
> Myself, my reputation;
> The lone way is my choice.

The second thing to be done is taught in the
next requirement made by the Saviour on this
night of gracious miracle: " Draw out now, and
bear unto the governor of the feast "—that is,
take the water filling the vessels and bear it to the
company as if it were wine.

Here is faith. When a man consecrates—fills

10

the vessel to the brim—he is then to believe that
Christ does the work, changes the water into wine,
and in evidence of faith actually dips it out and
hands around his experience.

Christ said to the nobleman: " Thy son liveth."
He believed, and returned home resting on the
word.   The lepers believed the word of Jesus, and
walked away toward the temple to show themselves and present the offering of clean men.
What wonderful faith in both instances!   Here the
servants are required to draw out and bear away
water as wine to the people at the table, before
they have opportunity to taste and see for themselves.   They were not allowed to have the witness of taste, but made to depend on Christ's
word.   The man seeking holiness, or the wine experience, must fill his vessel up to the brim with
the water of regeneration and a full consecration,
believe in his soul that Christ turns the water into
wine, and declare his faith by drawing out and
bearing the new grace to any and all that may be
around.   This is not only faith but confession, and
confession we know is but faith talking.   " With
the heart man believeth unto righteousness, and
with the mouth confession is made unto salvation."

Let the reader fix his eyes earnestly upon these
sentences:

" Fill the water pots up to the brim."

" Draw out now."

" Bear unto the governor of the feast."

"And they bore it."

" The water was made wine."

"And the governor of the feast called the bridegroom, and saith unto him, . . . Thou hast kept the good wine until now."

These sentences are the boundary lines about the great blessing written about in this book. They are the walls shutting in the garden of Eden lost by Adam and restored to us by Christ. In their sweet encircling lies the beautiful life and experience of purity and perfect love. Let us go over the walls and possess it!

Let us press this thought in another way. If the reader who is panting after holiness will commence with the first sentence and go from one to the other in perfect obedience to their teachings and requirements, he is certain to obtain the experience and realize the consummating work of God in the soul.

Let the reader look at the sentences and ask where or at what time was the water turned into wine. Was it when the vessel was filled to the brim, or when drawn out, or when borne to the governor, or when poured out for him to drink?

Each one of these steps was essential, and somewhere between the first and the last the water suddenly blushed into wine. In order for the water of regeneration to crimson into the joyous wine of sanctification there must be a perfect consecration, perfect faith in the word of the Lord, obedience to his direction and confession of that faith, and a pouring out of testimony into any and every empty heart around. No step can be omitted and not a single one of the directions disregarded. Somewhere in there the blessing comes. Somewhere in there the water turns to wine.

The writer once saw a minister seeking the blessing of holiness; he "filled the vessel up to the brim;" the Spirit whispered, "Draw out now and bear." Immediately he obeyed, and looking at the writer said: "I have it." In this act and these words he was bearing to the Governor and to the crowd assembled. That same instant the water was turned into wine; and all of us agreed, as with spiritual palates we tasted what he poured forth, that with him as in the feast the best experience had been kept until the last.

CHAPTER XIX.

THE TREASURE AND THE PEARL.

THE two blessings are remarkably taught in the parables that bear the above names. The first character introduced is that of a wayfarer. He seems to be going on in a purposeless kind of manner, when suddenly as he is crossing a field he discovers buried treasure. Doubtless his foot had struck away some dirt or gravel that covered it, thereby disclosing something that aroused and incited investigation; when lo! as he commenced examining and digging, the buried chest of treasure burst on his delighted and expectant gaze. He flies back and with what he has secures the field in which the treasure lies. A field in the East is not much in size, and a small price secures its possession. And this the wayfarer immediately did.

He well represents the unconverted man suddenly stumbling upon salvation. The sinner is a wayfarer going along in an aimless way through life. Nothing is farther from his mind than the thought of the preciousness and proximity of salvation. He walks over it and about it constantly in

churches and amid religious gatherings, but fails to
see it for himself. He goes to church aimlessly;
he visits a camp meeting with no fixed purpose;
certainly the treasure of salvation is not dreamed of
as being found and owned by himself. In nearly
every instance the unconverted man suddenly discovers the treasure. Under some pointed sermon,
stirring prayer, or melting hymn he is brought in
a moment's time to conviction and the feet of
Christ. He, so to speak, stumbles on salvation.
The author recalls the case of a young man who
afterward became a prominent preacher. He was
riding along the road when his attention was at-
tracted by the sound of singing and by the sight
of a number of horses hitched near a church in a
grove. Dismounting, he entered the building, and
in a few minutes was under the most powerful
conviction through the earnest preaching of the
minister. At the end of the sermon he rushed
forward to the altar and in a few minutes found
salvation. In a word, a certain wayfarer crossing
a field of grace suddenly found therein the buried
treasure of salvation.

The second character who appears in the parable that follows was a merchantman. He was a
man of wealth, for he was a dealer in pearls.
Moreover, he was seeking pearls. On hearing

of a very superior pearl, he sold all that he had, and purchased it.

This merchantman is a true representative of the regenerated man, who is no poor, sinful wayfarer, but a child of God, rich in stores of grace. The Christian is a spiritual merchantman, owning moral wealth. All the fruits of the Spirit are in his heart. He owns pearls. Moreover, he is seeking pearls. Whatever is pure and true and good he is after. He is growing in grace and adding to his faith virtue, temperance, and all other precious, beautiful, and holy things in the spiritual life. As he thus lives he hears there is another grace or blessing that he has not yet obtained. He sees and hears allusions to it in books and sermons. The day comes when he beholds it flashing in the face and testimony of some child of God. At once his soul burns to possess it. He asks the price of the pearl of heart purity or holiness, and is told that it takes all that he is or has or can ever be to obtain it. At once he sells all and secures the beautiful, precious prize. The " all " that he lays down is name, fame, reputation, good works, time, talents, influence, family, future, and self. He sells out all and gets the pearl of great price, the experience of holiness. Truly it is of great price.

About this experience there are several remarkable facts that are suggested by the pearl itself as a figure or symbol.

One fact is that the pearl is much more easily carried than the treasure. Let the reader fancy the labor of the man lugging off his box of riches. Then glance at the man who moves along with the pearl of great price in his pocket. Does the reader realize that sanctification is much more easily kept than regeneration? What memories the writer has of trying to manage and take care of his religion! What views he has had of people in a great agony over their religious experience, even as a man would strain and haul at a box heavily weighted! Their experience seems like a load instead of a help as it should be. They drag it around. They haul it to camp meeting. They stand guard over it with much terror at times. Their religion seems to be a trouble to them. Now look at the person who has sold all he had, and now has in his soul the precious pearl of purity. The heaviness and anxiety seen in the other life is altogether gone. How lightly and easily the man moves along! The whole of the Christian life seems to have been condensed in the blessing of holiness. Religion has been simplified. The blessing comprises all. Every duty and joy

can be found in holiness, as all the possessions of
the merchantman were swallowed up in the pearl.
How easily and how swiftly a man can move
through life and about God's service with the
pearl experience of heart purity!

Another fact that impresses itself is that the
pearl is hidden. A man does not carry a pearl as
he would a pebble. It is generally secreted in the
clothing. So the blessing of holiness is, in a
sense, hidden. Paul speaks of the hidden life.
John talks about the white stone with a new name
which no man knoweth saving he that receives it.
The concealment does not arise from the fact that
those who enjoy the blessing will not declare it,
but that as a work of grace it is hidden from
many eyes. For some reason they cannot see
the pearl of great price which has made us
rich and brought an indescribable gladness to our
lives.

If we take it out and show it to them, it is still in
a sense hidden. Many refuse to believe it is a
pearl. They say it is a mere fancy or delusion on
our part.

Conceive of a person saying to the merchantman that he was deluded about his pearl; that it
was only a crystal or glass bead. But, mind you,
he was a merchantman and knew pearls, and

he had bought it from one who would not deceive him; and so he only smiled, pressed the
pearl closer in his hand, and went on his way rejoicing.

Exactly so do we feel and do when men say we
are mistaken about the experience of heart purity.
Thank God we understand religious experience
and the work of God from a freak of the mind!
We can tell a pearl from a bead, and holiness of
heart from a delusion. Above all, we know who
gave it to us, and that he would not deceive us.
The soul knows what it possesses, and so in the
midst of skeptical looks, smiles, and utterances we
go on clasping the proven experience to the heart,
and rejoicing as we go.

A third fact is the value of the pearl. It was of
great price. The entire property of the merchant
had gone into it, and it was a fortune in itself.
What did he care now for sinking ships and burning houses? Where was his anxiety about miss-
ing flocks and stolen treasure? He had his fortune on his person or in his hand.

The same exultant indifference to all earthly
losses and changes is seen in the man who enjoys
the experience of holiness. It is the one thing
needful. Comprising as it does purity of heart,
perfect love, unshaken faith, undisturbed peace,

and the constant indwelling of Christ, it is the all-essential and all-satisfying blessing of the soul. As it is the one thing needful, then all other things are not needful. Nothing else is essential to the soul's happiness and victory. Let the news come of destroyed house or store, of moneyed losses, of deserting friends and changing affection; let health give way and loved ones die—thank God the pearl is left. The one thing needful for happiness and usefulness and heaven abides within. The man is still unmistakably rich. It is a pearl of great price that is in the soul, and although everything else be taken from him, yet having that he goes on singing. He may be cast off by men, may be clothed in rags and die as did Lazarus, a beggar before the rich man's gate; yet is he truly the rich man, and goes up to God with a value in him beyond that of all the mines and treasure of the earth.

It can do what nothing else can. If the heart is unclean, not all the world, with its songs and books and plays and pursuits, can make that heart happy. But the pearl of heart purity can do what the world cannot. This world can turn against us, the songs may be hushed, its literature taken away, its people cast us out, its houses shut against us, and we be treated as though the mark of Cain

was upon us, yet having the pearl we have unshaken joy and exultation of spirit. The pearl
brings us all we desire. It purchases for mind
and soul all that they need. We lack no good
thing. Our cups are made to run over while God
prepares a table for us in the presence of our enemies. Truly it is a pearl of great price.

CHAPTER XX.

HERE is another remarkable typical teaching of the final work and completing grace of God in the soul.

Lazarus dead is a type of the sinner.

God elsewhere in his Word likens the unregenerated man to one dead in trespasses and sins. Here he is made to appear in the tomb. Truly the sinner is a dead man. Christ is near, and he knows it not; friends are grieving over him, but he fails to realize it. He is as insensible to the spiritual as a corpse is to the physical world.

If any one would know how dead the sinner is, just call upon him to forsake his sins and give his heart to God. Call aloud; call again; call still louder; tell him he is in danger; that death and the judgment are approaching, that life is flying, that character is forming, that Jesus is waiting. You have done so a thousand times already to brother, son, husband, and father. They do not hear you because they are dead. They do not reply because they are spiritually lifeless. Your words cannot reach them. There is but one voice

that can. How we ought to love him who alone
can wake our beloved dead!

Lazarus brought to life is the type of the regenerated man. What an hour that was when Jesus
approached the door of the sepulcher to call forth
the man who had been dead four days. The Saviour spoke twice before raising him. First he said
to those standing around: "Take ye away the
stone." There is something the Church has to do
before Christ will do his work. There are stones
of indifference, coldness, stiffness, and worldliness
that we have to remove from the individual and
Church life before sinners can be raised from the
dead.

Again he spoke: "If thou wilt believe, thou
shalt see the glory of God." This was said to the
sisters. There is a select circle to whom Christ
looks to create an atmosphere of faith in which he
would operate. He does no mighty work where
there is unbelief. He is to-day, as then, waiting
for our faith in order to do marvelous things. If
we believe in Him and his power, we will always
see the glory of God.

Now then are heard the words: "Lazarus, come
forth." And he that had been dead came forth.
O how that voice pierced the dull, cold ear of
death! "Lazarus, come forth!" The reader

will remember how that same voice reached his
soul. It was heard in sermon, hymn, or prayer,
and somehow found entrance into the soul. You
listened, it moved you, it seemed to call you by
name, and it said, " Come forth," and you came.
Lazarus had been dead four days. How long
had the reader? The author had been dead
twenty-six years when that voice penetrated his
ear and reached his soul. Is it likely that a man
will ever forget the sensation of that sweet, new
life, as it rushed into his spirit at this time? The
soul came forth from darkness, sin, and corrup-
tion into light, life, love, and joy. It is not difficult to imagine the awe, wonder, delight, and
gratitude that fills the people round about when he
that was dead stands alive in their midst. It is at
such an hour that the hardest natures melt in seeing the rapture filling others at the sight of loved
ones brought to life by the power of God.

In building once a large camp meeting tabernacle the carpenter left a wide space between the
altar and front line of benches. The writer asked
him why he did so (this question being propound-
ed in his early ministry, before he had seen many
like Lazarus raised from the grave). He replied
that it was to " give room for friends and relatives
to embrace." We smiled then, but have often

since had our eyes to fill as we have beheld just such scenes as he spoke of. O the Marys and Marthas we have seen throw themselves on the breast of one who had been dead ten, twenty, thirty, forty years, and had been brought to life by the word and power of the Lord Jesus Christ! Yes, we say with the carpenter, " Give them room."

Lazarus set free is the type of the sanctified man. The dead man had been made alive, but the Gospel says he was bound hand and foot with grave-clothes. It was after a distinct interval of time that the Saviour speaks the second time and says: " Loose him, and let him go." At once the bonds were taken from him, and the living Lazarus became free.

The writer cannot believe this was an accidental order of events, but thinks that all was done with a deep significance. Somehow it wonderfully fits into the experience of the sanctified. The regenerated man is alive, but who is ready to believe he is perfectly free? What is this that adheres to the spirit after conversion; that binds, limits, and restricts in various ways. The Christian is again and again made conscious of it in prayer, in religious testimony, in teaching, in preaching, in acts of duty, in confession of Christ, in difficulty of responding to religious calls, demands of the Spirit, and claims of the gospel for acts of great sacrifice.

There is a feeling of being bound up and bound down. There is a mournful consciousness of not being easy and free, as is our privilege. The explanation is to be found in spiritual graveclothes, the cerements of death that still cling to and hamper the living child of God, necessitating a second work of grace.

Look at the man! He cannot use his hands in clapping or waving them in joy and triumph; he cannot leap as David did. Something binds hands and feet, sensibility and faculty. He calls it sense of decorum, dignity, and other fine names. But they are graveclothes left clinging to the soul. He cannot shout and praise God in any company as did the apostles at Pentecost, because something ties the tongue and binds the jaws. He calls it by the pleasing name of temperament, disposition, and other fanciful titles; as if God would ever give a man a temperament that would keep him from praising aloud his God and Saviour. The real name of the bandage is man-fear, which has been woven and wrapped around the mouth and jaws by inbred sin and which has to be removed by a second command and touch of the Lord.

The unfriendly critic will say that the bystand-

11

ers removed the bandages from Lazarus; but the
critic overlooks the fact that Christ does the work
of perfect liberation by the Holy Spirit, and the
hands of friends are made here to typify the loving Agent whom he uses in our behalf.

"Loose him, and let him go." Does not the
reader know that Lazarus moved gladly and easily
forward after this? He did not need to be pushed
or dragged. Let him go, and lo! he went of
himself. Thus when the disciples were loosed on
the day of Pentecost they fairly flew. Threats of
Herod, hate of Sanhedrin, breadth of ocean,
weary length of land—none of these things could
stop them. They were loosed, and like the eagle
when freed springs away into the distant and diz-
zy blue sky; so these men with resistless might
and speed flew to the far-away nations where
souls were dying and God was calling. In a little
while their voices were heard in Italy, Greece,
Spain, Ethiopia, and India. No land was too far,
no difficulty so great as to discourage and check
these liberated spirits.

How the Church needs this freedom! The
graveclothes all off. Every hand and foot and
tongue liberated and set going for God and the
good of man. This is the blessing God's children
need to-day. To be loosed, unbound, and unfet-

tered in hand, foot, tongue, purse, and life. To
have taken off all wrappings and bindings. To
have flung away everything that confines and keeps
them from being perfectly free. And Christ can
do it, and declares with his own lips: "If the Son
shall make you free, ye shall be free indeed."

Reader, are you free, and free indeed? Is the
string that holds down the tongue cut? Is the clasp
that fastens the purse broken? Are the bandages
about the mouth, hand, and foot gone? Are you
loosed? And are you going on to Zion singing,
rejoicing, walking, running, and mounting up as
on eagles' wings?

"Let him go." If you have the blessing of
sanctification or spiritual freedom, you will go.
All the world cannot prevent you. No more drag-
ging of one's self to prayer and to church as a
wearisome task, but with a gladsome haste to do
the will of God. There will be a delightful meeting and fulfilling of duty, while members of body
and powers of soul in consecrated service are like
the wings of the cherubim in constant motion for
God.

The result of this gracious work on Lazarus
upon the minds of others was remarkable. Many
believed in Christ. And this will always be seen
when Christ carries on his twofold work of mak-

ing alive and setting free.   Others did not believe:
''But some of them went their ways to the Phari-
sees, and told them what things Jesus had done.''
Some people will not believe, although one should
be raised from the dead.   Some people, instead of
being melted, moved, and won by the sight of
Christ's work in pardoning and sanctifying, steel
their hearts against the marvelous vision and go
off to report the transaction with various verbal
additions, to the enemies of the holy work in question.

A great work had been done in Bethany, sufficient to have moved the hardest and blindest; and
yet look at yonder retiring band!   See their shaking heads; mark their conferring together; look
at them disappearing over the brow of Mt. Olivet
in hot haste for Jerusalem, not to magnify the
grace of God to its citizens, but to pour out their
unbelief and hate in the ears of prominent men
prejudiced like themselves.

Great miracles are still being done in the land:
Lazarus is not only raised from the dead, but set
free.   The blessing of freedom can no more be
denied than yonder bird's release from the hand
as it sings far up in the air.   And yet there are
those who, instead of rejoicing over the grace of
God in his liberated child, hie away to those prom-

inent in authority who are known to be unfriendly to the doctrine of sanctification, and report the whole occurrence with various additions, touchings-up, and mental colorings so that through the fault-finding tongue and the equally unfriendly ear a grave offense is seen where heaven had achieved blessings for earth and angels and men had been made to rejoice.

How often the writer has seen such people retire from an hour that had been rich with the grace of God, with heads together, excitedly conferring one with another, and finally disappearing together!

So disappeared the doubting band over the brow of Mt. Olivet. Nevertheless Lazarus was free!

CHAPTER XXI.

THE BREASTPLATE AND HELMET.

IN the sixth chapter of Ephesians and fourteenth verse Paul speaks of " the breastplate of righteousness." On referring to the Greek Lexicon we find the word "righteousness " to be the same used in 1 Corinthians i. 30, where it is said that Christ is " made unto us righteousness." It has in it all the meaning of the word " justification." The soldier of Christ is described by Paul as having on this covering and protection, together with girdle, shoes, and shield. These expressions, paraphrased and explained, mean that man in a justified condition, is supported by truth, goes on missions of peace, and lives a safe and sheltered life through faith.

Yet this is not enough for him, nor all that God has for him; so he is exhorted in the seventeenth verse to take the helmet of salvation; in other words, to go on to perfection or obtain the second blessing.

The second work of grace shines out beautifully in this connection. We call the reader's attention to several points: One is that the breastplated or

(166)

justified Christian is still in a decidedly vulnerable condition. That unprotected head is marvelously suggestive of weak and exposed points in the regenerated life. The touchiness, sensitiveness, and festering wounds that many carry are due to the unhelmeted state, or, in other words, to the fact that salvation has not covered all and done all it can do and is proposed of God to do for the believer. There is a conscious lack of full salvation in the breast of the converted, a lack evident to beholders, of some essential and crowning grace.

If any one should ask where the converted man is most easily reached and hurt, we would say: "On the unhelmeted head." From observation and experience we hazard the assertion that the regenerated suffer much through their tongues, get deeply wounded with Satan's arrows in the eyes, get shot in the ears, and are likewise much hurt in the region of the brain. Their intellects are continually being offended; their opinions of men, things, customs, doctrines, etc., carefully formed and hoisted up into the cerebral roof are constantly being wounded and cost them much pain because they have not yet received the work of grace which covers that part of the man.

The preaching of holiness nearly always wounds these brethren in the head. It either in its holy exactions strikes something in the mouths of the brethren, cigar, tobacco quid, snuff bottle, or filthy anecdote, or it assails some pet and cherished notion of the brain.   So that the head of a justified man is exposed both to the devil in his attacks and to the assaults of holy men of God.   Does not this fact argue the necessity of a second work?

A second fact that appears in the symbol is that there is a distinct interval of time between the breastplating and helmeting of the soldier.   In all countries and all ages the placing of the helmet in position comes after the other.   And in the kingdom of grace that which is typified by these symbols takes place in the same order.   Mr. Wesley says he never knew a man to be regenerated and sanctified in the same moment.   How far some Methodist people have drifted from the teaching of their founder and from the Word of God the reader is left to decide.   The true order is, first breastplated with justifying grace, and then afterward helmeted with sanctifying power.

A third teaching appears in the fact that the helmeting was an immediate operation.

The helmet was not swung up out of reach and the soldier told to grow to it; but it was brought to and instantaneously placed upon him.   How absurd it is for the Church to-day, after seeing to it that we have the breastplate of justification or regeneration, to place the helmet of full salvation out of present reach, and tell us to grow toward or up to it! Not so teaches the Bible; the word there is, "having put on the breastplate of righteousness," now "take the helmet of salvation." It is nigh to all. Any one can have it. Come and take it.

A fourth teaching in the passage is that the "helmet of salvation" stands for a superior blessing.

No one who understands armor will hesitate in saying that the helmet takes rank over the breastplate in value and importance. Its conspicuous position, its finished beauty, its waving plume—all declare its superiority.

No one who studies the blessing of sanctification, and sees what it is, and what it does; what beauty it has, how elevated its life, how prominently and clearly it shines from the face and burns from the tongue, but will say this is the superior and crowning grace of the Christian life.

The disciples had been breastplated with pardon and righteousness for years, but on the morning of Pentecost they were helmeted with full salvation. Just as the helmet is brought and placed on the head from above, so this completing work, this headpiece of salvation, was brought to them from the skies and placed upon them. O what glorious, full-panoplied soldiers of Christ they were as they moved around with plumes of celestial flame waving from the helmet of salvation which had just been placed upon them by the Holy Ghost! All Jerusalem flocked down to see the marvelous and resplendent spectacle. And to this day there is nothing in the kingdom of grace that so attracts the multitude and so excites the wonder and speculation of the people as the bestowment upon believers of the helmet of salvation. It is true, in these days, that God has made the plume of flame invisible, but its light is still reflected in the face, and its fire burns in the tongue as powerfully as of yore. The blessing of sanctification or the baptism of fire cannot be concealed any more to-day than it could two thousand years ago in the upper room in Jerusalem.

A fifth thought is that not until after the helmet is placed on the head is the sword of the Spirit given. Let the reader turn to the next chapter of Ephesians and see for himself.

This corresponds with the case of the disciples. They were allowed, in their breastplated life, to go forth for a few days at a time and handle the sword a little in some villages and against a few score of devils, just like one would allow an apprentice to practice awhile before taking full possession and charge of certain instruments and work. But it was not until the helmet of salvation was placed on their heads in the morning of Pentecost that the sword of the Spirit was, in a sense, fully given to them and they were turned loose on the nations and the world.

The command had been, " Tarry for the helmet of salvation; for induement of ' power from on high,' " before permission would be given to go forth handling the sword of the Spirit, which is the word of God. And the command is still the same to the Church: " tarry for the helmet;" don't go forth with the sword without it. Would that God's people would hear and obey. If they did, instead of wounds and failures and foiled weapons and uncertain " beating the air," striking no sin, failing to hurt Satan's kingdom, and realizing frequent defeats, there would be a ringing shout, a glorious advance movement, and blessed victory all along the line.

The apostolic Church, after obtaining the " helmet of salvation," seemed never to meet with a defeat. It was an unbroken triumph for years and scores of years, and so would the Church be victorious to-day if it obtained the gladness, power, and irresistible might that come in the reception of that crowning work of grace, called variously "sanctification," "the second blessing," "the baptism of the Holy Ghost," and here by the apostle, "the helmet of salvation."

A sixth thought is that when the soldier of Christ becomes fully armed or panoplied with salvation he becomes, in a sense, invulnerable or (if I may be allowed to coin a word that suits better) "unhurtable."

The trouble with many Christians, all will admit, is that they are always getting their feelings hurt, some one is continually grieving or wounding them. The consequence is that the Church to-day is like a hospital where the few saved ones are kept busy all the time waiting on the spiritually sick, morally hurt, and a large number whose "feelings are hurt" and sensibilities wounded.

We have thought of suggesting to some churches the propriety of having four "wards:" the first, for those wounded by fancied slights; the second, for those whose feelings have been grieved by something said in the sermon; the third, for those offended at not being visited enough; and the fourth devoted and set aside to "incurables." The next step would be to call for volunteer nurses, those who are willing to hang up the sword, quit the battlefield, and change from soldiers into nurses.

The trouble with these wounded ones is that they went into the battle without the helmet. They thought the breastplate was all that was needed, and as a consequence are always getting hurt, and most of the time are in the hospital.

To obtain the " helmet of salvation " is to become fully panoplied and so covered with the protecting power of salvation as to become in a blessed sense " unhurtable." The writer has read of knights of the olden time who were so incased with armor that the enemy could not reach them with a missile. Finding them on the field, they would hack and hew unavailingly until, cutting the strings of the helmet, they got access to a vital place, and then inflicted a deadly wound. So it is in the blessed life and experience of the genuinely sanctified. You can cut and thrust and strike and belabor, and all the while the man is rejoicing unhurt and untouched because clothed and armored with full salvation.

We remember once hearing a prominent preacher talking to a Conference, and in the course of his remarks he alluded to certain events that some thought were disappointments in his former ministerial life. Bending his head down until the top of it was visible to all, he touched it with his hand, and said: " Brethren, there is no sore place there! "

The reason was that he had worn the " helmet of salvation." Some sharp - eyed critic may say that there was no armor for the back mentioned by the apostle, and that the helmeted man might be wounded there. The reply is that God mentions no armor for the back because he never intended his soldiers to retreat!

Hence it is that with the breastplate of pardon, the shield of constant faith, and the helmet of full salvation, the man of God is covered, protected, and perfectly safe.

CHAPTER XXII.

THE TWO TABLES.

THE two tables referred to above are to be seen in Hebrews xiii. 10: "We have an altar, whereof they have no right to eat which serve the tabernacle."

The reader will remember in his old Testament reading that the Levites were appointed to serve the tabernacle; that not only their support, but their food was allotted to them by divine commandment. The priests outranked the Levites in the ministry, and were not only to be distinguished from them by their office and dress, but in the very food they ate. They were allowed certain parts of various sacrifices, and in this enjoyed a privilege and peculiar table of their own. He that doubts this statement is requested to read the seventh chapter of Leviticus and be convinced.

The meaning of Hebrews xiii. 10 now becomes evident. According to this passage there are two altars or tables at which God's people eat. In other words, there are two distinct experiences of grace in the Christian life.

The fact taught in the verse quoted above is

what may be seen all over the Church to-day. God's children are sitting down at two different tables.

Two tables in the paternal home is a fact known by Southern children. They were called the " first " and " second " tables. The writer sat at the second when a child, and has vivid recollections regarding its position, size, and possessions. It was not long before he made some important discoveries about the table where he and one or two others of his age and weight were placed. One was that there was not as much on the second as on the first; nor was there as much beauty of arrangement; nor was there the same kind of company. The father was kind, and sent us food; but he was distant, and it was difficult at times to gain his ear and get a message through. We lacked a number of good things that they had in abundance at the first table. Especially we noticed that conversation flowed and hilarity abounded with them, while we at the second table were rather disposed to be silent, and sometimes critical and severe at the expense of the guests, and elder brothers and sisters who were having so much better time than ourselves. But the day came when the wistful eye and ear and heart were to be gladdened and delighted by a dining-room translation. In some way we were told that if we would put on a spotless white apron, and keep it clean, and promise to behave ourselves, then we should be promoted from the second to the first table. Of course we promised.

Will we ever forget the pride and joy of the moment when suddenly we found ourselves transported to a table loaded down with good things, ashine with cut glass and silver, surrounded with nicely dressed people, sitting side by side with grown up brothers and sisters, and above all in touch and whispering distance with our father!

This was the second blessing at the old home. It certainly was and is a great blessing to have a seat at the second table of a Christian home; but to come to sit close to your father at the first table, in any company and at all times, is even better, and is indeed a second and a greater blessing.

A look into our churches to-day reveals the fact that God's children are sitting down at two different tables. Let us glance a moment at these two tables. We first notice the second: One thing that immediately strikes the observer is that the people sitting about it are disposed to be silent. There seems to be little or no conversation on deeply spiritual subjects. There is talk about Church matters and doctrinal subjects of a contro-

12

versial character, but little of what is called holy conversation. There is also a marked absence of joy.

We observe also that the cloth on the table becomes frequently soiled, and the people there are kept busy in cleansing it from stains. We notice that the table is not without bread, but some of it is stale, and that which is fresh does not seem to be much in quantity. In fact, the people sitting at the second table say that they are often hungry, that while sometimes they get more than usual, yet generally they arise from the table unsatisfied.

The next thing in view is a small vessel with milk, and a glass containing water. The goblet, however, is far from full; and our regenerated brother will observe that while it is sweet and good and refreshing, yet he does not seem to get enough, and is often tormented with an inward spiritual thirst and feels most of the time unsatisfied.

On the table we noticed a few bitter herbs, and one told us that all people eating at the second table got these at times in their lips, and then suffered much afterward with bitter tastes in their mouths and acrid burning in their breasts.

To the question if the Lord is with them, the reply is: " Yes, now and then. Sometimes he is at the head of the table, and we are filled with gladness; but suddenly He disappears and is gone for hours and days. Sometimes we see him at the table every day, and then again we miss him for days and weeks.''

At this juncture we looked up and saw the first table. The first thing we noticed was the bright-faced, happy-looking circle of people that surrounded it. Every one had a smile, a song, and a shout, and seemed to be running over with love, joy, and enthusiasm.

The table cover was spotless and by some gracious power was constantly kept clean and white. At the head of the board was the Saviour. The first table people told us that he was always there, that no day nor hour nor minute nor second found him absent; and that was one great cause of their gladness.

We saw that they had an abundance of bread, and also plenty of gospel meat. They remarked with great rejoicings that they did not know what spiritual hunger meant; that they were constantly filled and satisfied.

We saw in the center of the table a crystal vessel filled with the purest honey. They said that this dish gave to their spirits a delightful sweetness; that it seemed to them that a great lump of honey had been lodged in their souls and that it was dripping sweetness all the time, in their prayers, in their meditations, in their duties, and upon their whole life.

Instead of a glass of water, there was springing up by the table a beautiful crystal fountain, so that the souls abiding there knew nothing of spiritual deadness, dryness, or distressing thirst. A well of water springing up in the soul will hardly allow such a condition; but will create a freshness, gladness, and satisfaction in the soul both delightful and blessed.

In addition to all this there was a goblet overflowing with a wine made in heaven and such as was poured out for the disciples on the day of Pentecost. We remembered that on the second table they had barely a spoonful of this liquid, and being so small in quantity, it gave to the spirit a momentary glow and soon passed away. But here at the first table the wine was a striking feature, and flowed in abundance. The effect was something more than the transient glow seen at the second table, and amounted to spiritual intoxication, to downright religious drunkenness. Such a sight is rarely seen at the table of regeneration, but is constantly beheld at the table of sanctification. Those at the regenerated or second table look and wonder at the singing, shouting, and noisy gladness of those at the first table. They not only wonder, but criticize, doubt, and condemn. At the best they fail to understand.

But the secret is that at the second table there is but little of the wine of salvation, while at the first table the cups overflow with it. The one table cheers, the other exalts; the one refreshes, the other intoxicates. At the one we obtain sips, at the other great draughts; at the one a mouthful, at the other cups brimming and overflowing with the rich, strong wine of salvation.

It is impossible to be at the first table, with its cups running over with the wine of heaven, without getting drunk; and with the intoxication comes, of course, the singing, shouting, and language not always understood by those at the second table. The opinion of many criticisers is that the phenomena of the first table is to be accounted for by nervousness, animal excitement, peculiarities of temperament, etc. But the true explanation is to be found in the cup that is filled with the wine of salvation.

Bread and milk are the marks of the second table. But on the first we find honey to keep us sweet all the time, meat to give strength, and wine in such quantity as to fill us with singing and rejoicing continually.

God set this table four times in the book of Acts: once for the Jews in Jerusalem, once for the Samaritans in Samaria, again for the Romans in Cesarea, and last for the Greeks in Ephesus. In every instance they were filled and spoke with strange tongues. O how strange to some! While in the first instance the people charged it upon the disciples that they were drunk.

Up to June 1, 1889, the writer had been sitting at the second table for nearly fifteen years. But a little while before the date mentioned above, on looking around he discovered a company of God's people sitting at another and better table than his own. He saw that they had more of the bread of life, more of the water of life, more of the honey of the gospel, and that while he was drinking milk they were quaffing the wine of salvation and were filled with gladness. He observed their shining faces, heard their rapturous shouts, and his soul cried out to be with them and one of them. He was told by them that they had an altar or table whereof he had no right to eat unless he complied with certain conditions. The conditions were not unlike those exacted of him in childhood: that he must put on the white linen of the saints, keep it clean, behave himself, and obey every word of his Father; that if he did this he could be promoted from the second table to the first.

He promised, obeyed, and fulfilled every condition; and, glory to God, found himself at the first table, where he has been ever since, for over four years.

Thank God for the first table, where the soul never gets hungry nor thirsty! Abundance of bread gives strength, the " well of water " gives unfading and undying freshness to the soul, the honey keeps the spirit sweet, and the wine makes us shouting happy.

O that the Church would awake to its privilege and with one accord leave the second table and come up and sit down in heavenly places at the first table, where freedom and fullness, light and joy perpetually abound!

CHAPTER XXIII.

WALKING ON THE WAVES.

IN Matthew we have the wonderful night scene of Christ walking on the sea in the midst of the storm, beheld in fear by his disciples, and afterward received into the ship. The passage strikingly illustrates the regenerated life, together with the approach of the convicted believer toward, and his final obtainment of, the blessing of sanctification. We use the passage in the way of illustration.

"Tossed with waves." Here is a good description of God's children in this world. First one wave, then another, and still others rolling against and upon them as they resolutely set their faces toward duty and heaven. Christ has said go in yonder direction, and they are going, but tossed with the waves as they go.

"The wind was contrary." Who does not know this experience? Some days it is worse than others. Men are contrary, children and servants are contrary, influences of all kinds rise up and press with full force against the righteous course. It is felt in the pulpit, pew, and pastorate. It is

(184)

realized on the street, in the store, and at home. The wind began to be contrary with the first rising from bed, freshened to a stiff breeze by breakfast, and then became a gale all day. O that contrary wind felt so often in the regenerated life. How often it is that one can only hold his own without advancing, and still oftener is blown back to the port from whence he started!

I read once of a phantom ship that was seen steadily advancing over the waves in the face of a storm. The wind was dead against it, but it sailed calmly on. The sight filled the beholders with fear and awe. That same sight is reproduced in the sanctified life. The blessing of holiness enables a man to go steadily on in the face of contrary winds. Invisible breaths from heaven fill the sails of his life, and being far stronger than the opposing forces and storms of this world, the man thus impelled goes undeviatingly and unchangeably on in the teeth and face of the fiercest resistance that men and devils can arouse. The sight always fills with awe. It is felt to be supernatural, and is so. Let us mark well that sanctification does not stop contrary winds, but imparts a power superior to their wildest force.

"Toiling in rowing." St. Mark in his Gospel adds this touch to the already dark and painful

picture. There is many a true, regenerated preacher in the pulpit who knows the full meaning of this
toiling experience. There is many a child of God
whose hand is on the oar of duty, and to whom
spiritual duty is often felt to be a wearying labor.
The toilers in rowing in the Christian life are easily
recognized. A careworn, anxious look, the tired
expression, the nervous wrinkle in the forehead,
the drawn, set mouth proclaim the toiler. The Bible tells us of something better. Even history tells
of men singing as they row. The writer has seen
and heard for himself in regard to this last fact.
On the rivers of America, the lagoons of Venice,
and the sounds and bays by the sea men sung as
they rowed. But how long we labored with
strained mind and heart in the Christian life before we realized a second grace that put the word
"singing" in lieu of the other word, "toiling,"
and so changed the whole meaning of the sentence.

"Jesus went unto them." Christ appears at
this time to these disciples, as he has done to us all
in like circumstances. He comes because he is full
of sympathy and has relief for us. There never
was a Christian whose life was tossed with waves
and beset with contrary winds, and whose experience is that of a toiler in rowing, but Christ came

to that soul with promises of a higher and better experience. The fact that the heart yearns for it shows that the Saviour has been there with his promises.

"And the disciples were troubled, saying, It is a spirit." What a pity that Jesus is unknown in his approach to his people! This seems always to have been his lot, to be unrecognized; and the amazing fact still continues. He came to his own, and his own knew him not. He came on the waves to his disciples, and they were troubled and thought it was a spirit. He came to you in a dark night of sorrow and storm of trouble, and you did not recognize him. Christ approaches the Church with his dealings and his doctrines, and the Church has never, at first sight, known him. He wrapped himself in the mantle of redeeming love and stood among the people, and they did not know him. He threw around his form the doctrine of justification by faith, and a whole continent arose to reject him, saying it was not the Lord. He cast about him the doctrine of the witness of the Spirit, and vast bodies of Christian people, failing to see Christ in it, condemned, ridiculed, and rejected the long-suffering Comer. And now he has clothed himself in the loveliest robe in the wardrobe of heaven, even holiness, and comes to the Church concealed in the mantle of sanctification; and the people are troubled, cry out for fear, and declare it to be a spirit, a phantom, a wild fancy, anything rather than the loving Christ.

"And Peter said, Lord, if it be thou, bid me come unto thee on the water." Some eyes pierce this disguise; some hearts, like a polarized needle, turn tremblingly, wistfully, and prayerfully to the Saviour at this time, and in the depths of their soul hope and feel that it is Christ. Perhaps not a child of God but once or more has said: " I believe it is Christ; there is another blessing for me, a higher grace, a deliverance from all inner care and conflict. ' Lord, if it be thou, bid me come ! ' "

"And he said, Come." Christ is calling you, Christian reader. It seems strange to call you out into what seems darkness, and into what proves a storm; to walk into an experience that seems as difficult and as impossible as to tread upon water. Yes, that is true; but still he is calling in the face and in spite of all these things. Men are hearing the call all over the land to-day. It is reaching the ear of the preacher in the pulpit and the member in the pew, the business man in his office and weary-hearted women amid the drudgeries of home

life. And the word is the same to all: " Come."
He would not call if he did not desire us, and would
not command us to come if we could not do so.

"And Peter walked on the water to go to
Jesus." Of all things ever done by mortal man,
this is to my mind the most amazing. Abraham
going to a strange land, not knowing whither he
went, was a great act of faith, but he had the firm
ground under his feet. When Peter sprang from
the gunwale of the ship out into the night and upon
the face of the stormy sea, and began to walk on
the waves toward Jesus, there was then performed
an act of faith that outstripped everything in the
past, and that immediately lined the walls of heav-
en with rejoicing and applauding angels. To obtain the blessing of sanctification, a like surrender
and consecration of the body, and faith in Christ
is demanded of us. To obtain holiness and keep
pure thereafter every second, is to the mind like
springing out and walking upon the waves. And
yet Christ says "Come." And, blessed be God,
not only Peter, but a great number besides have
heard the call, left the ship, and are now walking
upon the waves. One cannot remain in the ship
and walk upon the water at the same time. I have
seen people holding on to the ship with one foot
and feeling the water with the other. Of course

the foot sunk, and they arose disgusted, saying: " I knew it! It is impossible to have a pure heart all the time; you are bound to sin; there is no such thing as sanctification." The thing to do is to spring out from the ship and stand on the waves. Then there will be a different experience, testimony, and history altogether. Never will the writer forget when, a few years ago, he leaped out from the ship through the storm into the dark, and trod upon and walked upon the waves to go to Jesus. O the thrill of joy that went through him when he discovered that he did not sink, that he was kept pure by the blood every second, that the invitation " Come " was not an empty sound and mockery, that the divine promise and faithfulness bore him up and he could walk joyfully and with an ever-increasing confidence upon the waves. So has he been walking, leaping, and running ever since. He would now rather walk on the water than on the ground. He prefers the miraculous upholding and moving upon what seems water to the world, the life of sanctification, than to stand where he once did on the dry ground of regeneration.

" But when he saw the wind boisterous, he was afraid; and beginning to sink." So Peter began to sink. Alas for him! Now listen to the people talking. "I told you so;" "a person may walk the waves a little while, but he must soon go down;" "look out for these high professors;" "better stay in the ship like the other disciples;" "it was a piece of arrogance anyway on his part;" "why should he attempt to do what the other eleven did not try?" "served him right," etc. So the murmuring went on and still goes on. It is vain to remind the people that Christ was on the waves and that he said "Come." This alone should silence every tongue, although every walker on the water sunk afterward and found the bottom of the sea.

We are glad the Bible tells us why Peter sunk. He saw the wind boisterous, he got his eye off Jesus and was looking at the waves and regarding the winds. Of course he began to sink. This is the explanation of every sinking heart and experience in the sanctified life. Reader, you once walked well. O how you trod in joy upon the waves! and then suddenly you began to take note of the opposition and ridicule. You heard the windy threats. You trembled at a new and huge wave of combined opposition that arose against you, and instead of keeping your eye on Jesus and stepping on the waves as you would upon the stone or wood block in front of your door, and mounting up still higher, you eyed the wave and began to sink.

"He cried, saying, Lord, save me." Thank God for prayer! How it rescued sinking Peter that night! How it has saved countless ones since, and will yet save! "Rejoice not against me, O mine enemy: when I fall, I shall arise; when I sit in darkness, the Lord shall be a light unto me." How deep have you sunk, dear reader? Are you down to the ankles? Have you sunk to the knees? Or to the loins? I thank God you still can call upon Jesus. He is there upon the very waves you have so much dreaded. He is not sinking. Send out a thrilling cry to him over the waves: "Lord, save me!" He will hear and come. Have you sunk still deeper? Have the waters gone over your head? Then lift your hand if the voice is gone, and wave a signal of distress to him. He sees you and will come to your help. Are you deeper still, and the hand cannot be brought to the surface? Then look to Jesus through the water, and the look will bring him and save you. "Looking unto Jesus" is salvation.

"And immediately Jesus stretched forth his hand, and caught him and said unto him, O thou of little faith, wherefore didst thou doubt?" Blessed be God for the swiftness of Jesus to save and restore us when we really pray! "Immediately" is a very precious word. The whole explanation of the sinking is given in few words to the restored disciple to guard him in the future: "Little faith;" "wherefore didst thou doubt?" Brother, why did you doubt? If you walked upon one wave, you could walk upon a million. If you are kept pure one minute, you can be all the years of your life, through the power of the Son of God. Why did you doubt? Is Christ dead? Has he lost his power? Say: "God helping me, I will doubt no more."

"And when they were come into the ship." That is, Christ and Peter. You thought Peter was gone; and then you thought he would never walk the waves any more; and you thought Christ would have to carry him into the ship. Not so. That faithful hand lifts Peter up again on the waves, and that reassuring voice brings back the flying faith, and now the disciple turns, and with his Master at his side walks over the water and enters with him into the ship.

So should it be with many who read these lines. Christ will hear your cry; his hand will lift you up again, and you will walk the waves once more by his side. Why not? That same hand lifted five different times John Fletcher, who had sunk

13

through doubt four times. After the last rescue he walked with Christ into the ship.

The writer has a blessed vision of many, who through opposition and discouragement have sunk to various depths, coming up out of those depths! Christ is on the sea. " His voice is upon the waters." His hand will find the sinking one. And I see them, all glory to God, walking together on the waves, conversing side by side through the night and mounting up the billows as upon a stairway, and stepping at last on board the ship.

" The wind ceased." There is always a blessed rest after a great spiritual victory. The instant Christ enters the ship that has been tossed with contrary winds there is a great calm. This is felt in gracious measures now and then in the regenerated life; but is realized in its fullness and all the time in sanctification.

"And immediately the ship was at the land whither they went." This remarkable fact is stated only by John. But it covers an experience well known to all Christians, but especially, and in a far deeper sense, to the sanctified. How delightful suddenly to find yourself in the spiritual life where you have long desired to be, and in the possession of an experience for which you have been toiling unavailingly for years. To be sanctified is to suddenly find yourself where you have been longing and praying and striving all your life to be, it is in the deepest sense of the word to find yourself at the land and in a haven of profound rest and blessedness.

CHAPTER XXIV.

THE TWO PROPHESYINGS.

IN the first ten verses of the thirty-seventh chapter of Ezekiel we have the prophet's vision of the valley of dry bones. These bones were seen suddenly to come together, become clothed with flesh, then came breath, and they stood an exceeding great army covering the plain and hillsides.

There have been various explanations of this wonderful scene. Some think that the restoration of Israel is here taught; others, that it typifies the resurrection; and others claim that it is a picture of the work of salvation. Thus men are dead in trespasses and in sins, but through prophesying or preaching of the gospel they are brought to life. Some might contend that it stands for the reclamation of a backslidden Church, for the bones are described in the words, "these bones are the house of Israel." Moreover, a skeleton declares former life. The backslider is the skeleton of his former spiritual self, and his present state is one of dryness and death.

Let this be as it will, the work represented in the passage is that of salvation, and the only point desired to be made in this chapter is that there were two prophesyings in the valley of a distinct and different character before the great result seen in the conclusion of the paragraph was beheld.

The first prophesying was to the dry bones. This is a true description of preaching to the spiritually dead. Certainly at times it looks like a man might as well go out and speak to dry bones bleaching on the hillside. Alas that there are so many valleys thus filled! A church building is not unlike a valley with its four walls towering up like hills, with the sloping auditorium floor like a plain covered oftentimes with people in whose faces there seems not a particle of spiritual life. If here and there is seen a living one, the very sight makes the contrast the greater, with the dead all around.

To these dry bones the prophet or preacher is called upon to prophesy. What a command! How apparently hopeless the labor! What need to talk to dry bones? And yet this is the command of heaven. Speak to them just as if they were living creatures instead of being dead.

This is the test and sharp trial of the man of God. It calls up all the faith he has, to face such valleys filled with the dead on Sabbath days, and in the beginning of revival seasons and thus speak.

The direction as to what to prophesy or speak is

given. " Say unto them, O ye dry bones, hear the word of the Lord." It is the word of God that is to be spoken. Vain and resultless will be any other word. The only hope for dry and lifeless souls is the truth of God. O hearts dead in tresspasses and sins, listen to the word of God.

Then appears the result. The very thing, indeed, we see in every genuine revival of religion.

" There was a noise."

Of course there is and always will be a noise when something is being done. When devils are being cast out, the dead raised, and sinners saved there is bound to be a noise. There will be sobs of penitential grief, cries for mercy, and shouts of joy over sins forgiven. Of course there will be a noise, and one that Heaven will inspire and be pleased with. The Church in which the Holy Ghost abides and works is not like a silent graveyard, but resembles more a military camp, full of life, bustle, song, shout, and glorious achievement.

"And behold a shaking."

Yes, of sinners trembling to see themselves for the first time as they really are, and trembling of devils who realize they are being cast out by One able to send them into the pit which they so much dread.

"And the bones came together."

Truly it is so in a revival. There is fellowship and restoration, and everything else that should be and that has not been.

" The sinews and the flesh came up upon them, and the skin covered them."

There was a growth and improvement all the while—just what should be in every one who hears and receives the word of God and has been translated from the form of death into the form of life.

" But there was no breath in them."

Something was lacking. And that something required a second prophesying or preaching to obtain. Who has not felt that lack who has been raised from spiritual death? It is the confession of all honest regenerated men. In the face of all that God has done for them through his word and power they need something else. And it is felt to be as desirable and necessary as breath itself.

The second prophesying was unto the wind.

The wind here refers to the Spirit. Christ likened the work of the Holy Ghost to the wind. And on the day of Pentecost, you remember that he came as a rushing wind.

" Then he said unto me, Prophesy unto the wind."

Why not again to the dry bones? Because they

had disappeared, and a new work is to be done altogether.

Why a second prophesying? Because herein is indicated that God has two distinct messages to the soul: one concerning its arising from spiritual death, and the other its reception of the Holy Ghost.

The second prophesying the reader observes is to the wind, and not to the bones. Just as in the economy of salvation we leave the first principles and go on to perfection, so having received forgiveness of sins we tarry at Jerusalem and look up for the descent or baptism of the Holy Ghost.

The Church to-day is content with the first prophesying. They are satisfied with the first work while God's voice rings out in the command to prophesy unto the wind for the obtainment of this second work, a command that is the counterpart of Christ's instruction to tarry until the enduement of power comes from on high.

The book of Acts is devoted to that second prophesying. For ten days the disciples looked up awaiting the blowing upon them of the heavenly wind. John and Peter were sent to Samaria to tell those whom Philip's preaching had raised from the dead to look for the wind of heaven or the baptism of the Holy Ghost; while Paul, going among the Churches, asked with anxiety the question, "Have ye received the Holy Ghost since ye believed?"

"And the breath came unto them."

The reader is here directed to John xiv. 16, 17, where the difference between " with " and " in " is made to appear: "And I will pray the Father, and he shall give you another Comforter, that he may abide with you forever; even the Spirit of truth; whom the world cannot receive, because it seeth him not, neither knoweth him: but ye know him; for he dwelleth *with* you, and shall be *in* you."

The breath came into them. This is what happened to the disciples on Pentecost; what took place in Samaria under the second prophesying of John and Peter after the preaching of Philip; what occurred in Cesarea to the devout Cornelius; and what transpired at Ephesus to the twelve disciples under the preaching and praying of Paul.

The point may be made that according to Ezekiel's statement the dry bones did not live until the breath came into the bodies. The reply to this is found in Deuteronomy xxx. 6, where we find that it is not at birth, but, remarkable to say, after circumcision (which Wesley teaches stands for sanctification) that the soul is said to live. Of course the idea is not that there had been no life before ; but such an incoming power, such an uplift of grace has been realized that life is now seen in its highest enjoyment and expression.

" They stood up upon their feet."

We need just 'such a blessing in the Church to-day, and there is such a grace.   Paul speaks of it in Romans v. 2 : " By whom also we have access by faith into this grace wherein we stand?"   The idea is that after the second work of grace the Christian ceases to be the sitter and lounger in the kingdom.   That blessing makes one spring to his feet and stand in his place in the ranks of God's army ready for action.   Alas for the recumbent forms in the Church to-day!   The sitters, waiters, resters, and slumberers constitute the great body. O for the wind from heaven to come upon them, that they might stand, and having done all, to stand !

"An exceeding great army."

Holiness is going to win.   Christ came to sanctify his Church, and will do it in spite of men and devils.

A gentleman once saw a large body of soldiers sleeping on a plain.   A snow falling during the night had covered them, when just at break of day a bugle sounded, and suddenly the slumbering regiments, leaping up in every direction, stood revealed on their feet as a great army.

So vast multitudes seem to be resting or sleeping in the Church to-day. They are snowed under with formality. But the apocalyptic angel has set his trumpet to his mouth and is blowing. People are hearing the sound and are leaping into a life of spiritual joy and power everywhere. As the call increases in loudness and penetrates the ears of myriads who have not yet heard, there will soon be seen standing up for holiness in all the Churches just what Ezekiel saw in his vision: an exceeding great army.

CHAPTER XXV.

THE TWO BAPTISMS.

THAT man has read carelessly indeed who has not seen in the Word of God two distinct baptisms: the one of water, the other of fire.

The Holy Spirit is typified by both elements, while at the same time distinct works of the Spirit are brought out by the words "water" and "fire." John is clear on the subject when he says: "I indeed baptize you with water unto repentance ['for the remission of sins.' Mark i. 4]: but he that cometh after me is mightier than I, . . . he shall baptize you with the Holy Ghost, and with fire." (Matt. iii. 11.)

Under the preaching of the Baptist many received remission of sins. The Gospel declares that they were baptized, confessing their sins. It is impossible to believe that the pardon of these sinners was withheld and their salvation delayed for months until they saw Christ. To repent, confess sin, and obey God is to obtain forgiveness in every land and in every age. This fact was affirmed by Peter in his visit and sermon to Cornelius, while Mark is clear in stating in the first

(204)

chapter and fourth verse of his Gospel that the people obtained in John's baptism remission of sins. But immediately after this John cried to those thus blessed: "There is something better for you; there is another baptism to come; it is one of fire."

There are some facts noticeable about the baptism of fire:

Fire Destroys.—So does water, for that matter, but not like fire. A city overwhelmed by a flood is one thing, but destroyed by fire is another. The last far surpasses the first. The waters of regeneration sweep away one's personal sins; but there remain pride, self-will, ambition, and many other things still in the soul. Let the fire of sanctification fall and they will be utterly consumed. Carnality, the love of the world, the fear of man, the lust that survived the waters of regeneration will go down under the fire of sanctification.

Fire Purifies.—Regeneration is a cleansing work, but there is another and deeper one that the Scripture calls the "baptism of fire." The Saviour referred to the two works when he said to his disciples, "now are you clean through the Word;" and a little while after prayed to his Father, "Sanctify them." The purification by fire is deeper than the other, and indeed is perfect. You may take a piece of gold or iron as it is dug from the earth, and wash it thoroughly with water, and say truly that it is clean; and yet it is not pure because of the dross adhering to and within it. Let it now be treated to a washing or baptism of fire, and the dross is separated from it and the pure metal remains.

In regeneration the soul is clean as the washed iron ore is clean, but in sanctification it is pure as the metal is pure when the dross has been taken out. Isaiah refers to the first of these baptisms when he says that under it the heart becomes as "white as snow;" but David speaks of the second when he prays, "Wash me, and I shall be whiter than snow." God illustrates the two baptisms on a large scale by the globe itself. He once gave this world a baptism or deluge of water. It wonderfully cleansed the earth. The giants and monsters of iniquity and the daughters of men who were sinful and the mockers of Noah were all swept away from the face of the earth. It was a cleansed world. But behold carnality floated in the ark and cropped out after the disembarkation in the drunkenness of Noah and the mocking spirit of Ham. The next time God cleanses the world it will be by fire, and the flames will go round the globe in mighty billows like the waves of the deluge once went before. It will be a marvelous baptism, and the effect will be glorious. The Bible says that after this baptism of fire our earth will be a world wherein dwelleth righteousness. Sin will be gone and appear no more forever. No more giants of evil and moral monsters, no more drinking Noahs and jeering Hams, but angels and the redeemed will people the earth and God will dwell with them.

God has two baptisms or cleansings for the soul; one is regeneration, the other is sanctification. The washing of regeneration is one thing, the baptism of fire another. In regeneration there is a personal cleansing, but there is something still left in the ark that is wrong and that will evince itself some day; some mocking Ham or stumbling Noah principle or nature abiding within and bound to appear. In sanctification this is removed, and there comes down upon the man a purification by fire in which the heart is cleansed from all filthiness and becomes a spiritual world wherein dwelleth righteousness.

Fire Transforms.—A person can take an iron poker, cold, rusty, and unattractive; and placing it in the fire, it becomes like the fire. So let the soul be enveloped and filled with the heavenly flame of the blessing we are writing about, and the transformation is remarkable. A man is never so much like Christ as when the baptism of the Holy Spirit and fire is upon him. The coldness, stiffness, rustiness, unattractiveness are gone, and his words, bearing, and life are heavenly. It was after this baptism that the people took knowledge of the disciples that they had been with Jesus.

Fire Generates Power and Action.—We need not take time to show this to be the case in the mechanical and natural world, but simply show it as an existing fact in the spiritual life. When the baptism of fire comes upon the child of God he rushes away on Heaven appointed and directed lines of work. Steam is up, power has been generated, the throttle is wide open, and he goes flying down the road that God has cast up for him. After the fire fell on the disciples they flew to every land. When it came upon the early Methodist preachers they went everywhere seeking to save the lost. When it came upon Caughey and Finney and Inskip they burst away from municipal and State boundaries and swept over the entire land with flaming souls and tongues of fire. Did the reader ever notice that whenever a person catches on fire he invariably runs? So let the soul take fire, and with the holy baptism, the life of devoted service to God and man commences anew, never to end this side of the grave.

The Baptism of Fire Is God's Anointing for Service.—We are not qualified to work with and for souls until we possess it. Hence Christ told the disciples to tarry until it was obtained. All who have been successful soul winners speak of an experience of qualification or anointing of fire. After that they discovered a heavenly wisdom, a Christlike patience, an unflagging zeal, a strange power to melt and draw and win souls to God.

The great mistake of the Church has been in attempting the conquest of the world without this power. Nearly two thousand years of labor and failure to bring the world to Christ, with two-thirds of the race still ignorant of the Saviour, is a fact sufficient to send us to our closets, to upper rooms, and to churches, in days and nights of prayer, to ask for and receive the blessing that can alone make us irresistible and victorious. The word has been and still is: " Ye shall receive power after that the Holy Ghost has come upon you."

O for the fire! O that the Church would weep and pray before God until the flaming baptism of heaven would descend!

> O that it now from heaven might fall,
>   And all my sins consume!
> Come, Holy Ghost, for thee I call;
>   Spirit of burning, come.

14

CHAPTER XXVI.

THE TWO TOUCHES.

IN the gospel of Mark we read of a blind man whom Christ led out of the town in order to perform upon his sightless eyes a gracious miracle. Twice the Lord laid his hands upon him before his sight was perfectly restored. This incident is a complete refutation of the idea advanced that God does all for us in a single work. That the Lord need not go over his work through lack of power to do as he will, we admit; but that he does so is seen in the case of every reclamation of the backslidden, while the assertion that God does all for the soul in a single work of grace called regeneration is contradicted by voices and facts heard and seen in nature, providence, and grace. The creation of the world occupied not one, but six days, requiring not one, but six touches of divine power. The creation of the human family was not completed in the making of Adam, but in the second touch that produced Eve, who became the second blessing in the garden of Eden. There were two covenants given to the world, and the Bible says distinctly that the first was not perfect, but the second was. The Saviour himself on the

(210)

banks of Jordan received an anointing and baptism that he had not previously received. From this time he went forth in the power of the Spirit. Why did not this happen at his birth? Does not God do every thing in one work? Verily this scene on Jordan, and the other facts alluded to, say: " No! "

So we see that the miracle on the blind man wrought in two touches is in perfect harmony with these other teachings, and goes to establish the fact of a subsequent and completing work of grace.

The first touch on the blind man's eyes brought sight. He looked up and said: " I see." So said we all when the regenerating hand of God was laid on our souls. How sweet the light! how delightful the experience of coming out of darkness, and seeing spiritual truths and enjoying heavenly experiences! However, it was a defective sight. Like the man in the gospel account, we saw men as trees walking. This was certainly an alarming sight, and brings out clearly the man-fear and man-exaltation that is left in the heart. A man of wealth or position in the State or Church is as tall as a tree. There is a feeling of uneasiness and dread as he comes walking around. The soul instinctively dodges and runs. Who would not run from a tree walking around.

The second touch on the eyes brought perfect sight. The gospel says the man looked up and saw clearly. It is the second touch of grace realized in sanctification that brings a clear and proper vision of things to the soul.

We see into the Word of God as never before. Passages that were obscure and mysterious become luminous with a deeper and truer meaning. The Bible becomes a new book, and an illuminated edition at that.

We see into God's providence clearly. Occurrences that formerly disturbed, distracted, and alarmed us do so no longer. The clearer vision reveals Christ present everywhere and all the time, and also the blessed fact that all things are working together for our good. No combination of men or devils can paralyze or overwhelm the sanctified soul. That second touch enables him to see their impotency and the great power of God overarching all their designs and overruling all their works for the good of earth and heaven.

We see men clearly. There comes a spiritual discernment in sanctification that is astonishing. Of course no one claims infallibility of judgment, but an increased power to discern spirits and spiritual things that is self-protective and necessary as well for the peace, safety, and advancement of Christ's kingdom.

We see men as they really are. Not as trees walking; not as giants to be dreaded and fled from, but as men six feet high and just so many inches through from breast to back. It is marvelous how man-fear departs under the second touch of grace. It is delightful to be able to speak with and preach before the highest and richest in Church and State without tremor of nerve or sinking of heart. The writer has seen a field telescope shut up to its proper portable dimensions of six inches. So sanctification places a hand on a man's head and another under his feet; and then, so to speak, suddenly collapses or condenses him to his proper size, diminishing him from one hundred to six feet.

We see men as they really are, not as dwarfs. sanctification does not belittle a man. It does not view with contempt God's work and creatures. While the second touch shows us that a man is no giant, it also saves us from falling into the opposite extreme judgment and prevents us from regarding him as a dwarf.

The teaching of holiness is that a man is neither a tree nor toadstool. He is neither to be dreaded nor despised. He is a man, and as such is to be honored and loved. Thank God for the second touch!

CHAPTER XXVII.

CISTERNS AND FOUNTAINS.

THE two words forming the caption of this chapter well describe the difference of experience in regeneration and sanctification. A cistern is a receptacle whose contents are continually sinking, and which has constantly to be refilled. A spring or fountain, on the contrary, has connection with inexhaustible subterranean rivers, and is always full, always overflowing, and always the same.

We have only to look around in the Church to see that the cistern experience is the prevailing one. Many either have not heard of or do not care for a better experience.

Christ promises the fountain experience to all who will have it. He spoke to the woman of Samaria and called it a " well of water springing up;" and on the last day of the feast he promised it publicly, and revealed it flowing from the soul or inner parts as "rivers of living water." The reader will bear in mind that rivers take their origin from springs or fountains. John says: "This spake

(214)

he of the Spirit, which they that believe on him should receive: for the Holy Ghost was not yet given; because Jesus was not yet glorified.''

So the fountain experience is one subsequent to regeneration, '' they that believe on him should receive.'' It is to follow and displace the cistern experience. The man's soul is to be changed from a mere receptacle of blessings to a gushing fountain of grace. Instead of needing to be filled all the time, it is filling others. Instead of a pond existence, that has to be visited to be seen and to derive benefit therefrom, the life is to be like rushing rivers of living water going out in every direction, cheering, blessing, and saving the people.

The disciples were cisterns for three years and a half, but on Pentecost Christ transformed them into fountains. After that how they watered the Church, the people of Jerusalem, and the surrounding nations!

Many who read these lines will bear witness to the fact of the cistern experience: a religious life that is continually being emptied. A smaller number will testify to the fact that on learning of a better experience they came to Christ, and in the blessing of sanctification they have had an artesian well set up in their souls which has been flowing ever since.

The following are some of the advantages of the sanctified life, or the fountain experience.

One is that it is a constant experience of freshness. Spiritual barrenness and deadness cannot abide in the soul where a spring of life is flowing. A newness and freshness comes upon the heart that is not only delightful in itself, but gives a charm to life, to the world, to duty, and even to pain and suffering that cannot be described and certainly cannot be understood by one not in the blessing.

Again; it is an experience of abiding inward satisfaction. Just as a spray of water constantly playing upon the tongue and throat would allay and prevent thirst, so this artesian well of salvation springing up in the soul puts an end forever to the old dry hungerings and thirstings of spirit that fill the life with uneasiness and pain.

Again, it is an experience of conscious fullness. In the cistern experience we are continually alarmed to find the water of life low down in the heart or maybe all gone. More than once the writer has ceased from his pastoral visiting when a regenerated man, and with a painful sense of increasing emptiness would take the cars, go to his room, get on his knees, put up the troughs, and call on God for showers of grace to fill the empty vessel. But in the sanctified life or fountain experience there is a constant delightful sense of fullness. The heart does not run dry. The soul does not become empty.

Besides this there is the feature of inexhaustibility. Just as a spring runs steadily through the day and all through the hours of the night, so in the blessed life we speak of there is a steady flow all the while of religious life and power. The demands on the fountain for water no more exhaust the fountain than do the demands of men upon the sanctified person diminish his life and grace and joy. The artesian well of salvation flows on and up and out continually. The sense of spiritual exhaustion departs. Silence may fall upon the lip, and meditation occupy the mind, but the " well " is still flowing within and springing up into eternal life.

The last feature of the fountain experience is that such a life creates rivers of blessing, that flow in every direction, to the gladdening, enriching, and saving of souls. The cistern only gives as it is drawn from and pumped out; but the fountain flows over and runs out all the time. It is this last experience that is wanted to-day. A life that flows over and flows forth to others is the true and best life. A blessing that cannot be contained is the blessing that the Church needs to-day, for the sake of itself, and for the sake of the outside world. Give the fountain experience to the Church, and rivers of living water of blessing and of salvation will flow out in every direction to the human race.

CHAPTER XXVIII.

SERVANTS AND FRIENDS.

THESE two relations are well known in life and also prevail in the kingdom of Christ. The very terms appearing in the caption of this chapter were used by the Saviour and are to be found in John xv. 15: "Henceforth I call you not servants, for the servant knoweth not what his lord doeth: but I have called you friends; for all things that I have heard of my Father I have made known unto you."

There are two relations to Christ in the spiritual life. This is the teaching of the Lord himself and a fact confirmed by the experience of the heart, and by a faithful observation of the lives of God's people. There is a striking difference between servants and friends. We see this in the social life of the world, and we see it as remarkably in the Christian life.

One difference is that a servant serves for wages, but a friend serves for love. The first interview between the employer and employed is a stipulation in regard to price for labor rendered. But no deeper pain could be inflicted than to ask

(219)

a friend what he expected in the way of compen-
sation for doing a service. Think of a husband
asking a wife what she charged for sitting up all
night with him in his sickness. There is a hire
service in the Christian life; there are many who
serve God for blessings, sweet experiences, and
rewards. But there is such a thing as promotion
from a servant to a friend. In sanctification the
servant becomes a friend, and labors for Christ
from pure love. If there are no delightful experiences, no great spiritual blessings, he works on
just the same. If favors and promotions are not
bestowed, he does not become sour nor complain,
but keeps on laboring for the Master with the
same gladness and cheerfulness that a wife ren-
ders in the home of the unnoticing and absent
husband. It is a work of love.

A second difference appears in that the servant
knoweth not what his Lord doeth, while his friend
does. There are many things we tell a friend we
would not dream of communicating to a servant.
This is unquestionably the explanation of much
ignorance in regard to God and spiritual things in
the ranks of Christians. They prefer to remain
as servants, and so know not what the Lord doeth.
Much in the Bible is a mystery and many things
in Providence are misunderstood; but with the

elevation from a servant to a friend there comes a knowledge of divine truth, a recognition of the divine leading, an understanding of the divine mind, and a full and free communion with the divine Being that makes an epoch in the soul's history as wonderful as conversion, or birth into the kingdom. Christ says about this: "I have called you friends; for all things that I have heard of my Father I have made known unto you." Christ tells the friend all. Let the reader look and see in confirmation of this fact how the servants of Christ are running to the friends of Christ to be instructed more perfectly in the things of God.

A third difference is seen in the matter of a free and easy access to the Lord and Master.

The servant has to be summoned, has to tap at the door, and is constantly confronted with restrictions of approach and conversation. The friend comes when he will, and passes in and out with a freedom that is delightful. There is an openness, an assurance, a tender familiarity that is unknown to the other relation.

We have only to do some remembering or some observing to see many of God's children limited and restricted in their approach to and communion with God. They are not at ease with God. The voice declares distance, the language reveals a lack of perfect understanding. They are rapping at the door. The object of their love is not always in sight.

But there are others who, under the sanctifying grace of God, have become friends. Their very tones, words, spirit, and life declare intimacy with God, freedom of speech, ease of access, and thoroughness of understanding. These are the people that men go to and say: " Pray for me." These are the persons to whom people come with open Bible or with their troubles and say: " Please explain this to me."

The servant goes to the friend and says: " Bring me to the Lord and Master."

Who would not prefer to be the friend of Christ?

CHAPTER XXIX.

THE TWO COMPANIES IN HEAVEN.

ACCORDING to the seventh and fourteenth chapters of Revelation, there are two companies of redeemed people in heaven. The fact of two distinct bands is the striking thought of these passages of scripture; for while both are saved and in glory, yet there is a difference between them plainly observable.

There is no question about the identity of the "multitude that no man could number." These are evidently the vast hosts who in life and at death have believed on the Son of God and been saved. No man can number them, says the Word; and it is true. These are the regenerated, out of every land and kindred and tribe and people. They are washed in the blood of the Lamb.

But who and what is this other company of 144,000? Many have hazarded opinions; and if others have done so, why may not the writer try to interpret, if he does so humbly and reverently.

Some suppose that this company stand for those Jews who believed on Christ in the first century. But why confine it to the first hundred years? And what is there so different in the faith of a Jew and a Gentile as to create this marked distinction we see in heaven?

Some have suggested that the 144,000 stand for little children. They base their supposition on the expression that these "were not defiled with women."

Two facts show up the absurdity of this idea: One is that nearly one-third of the human race die in childhood, and as we know that children are saved, the 144,000 utterly fails to be a proper symbol of the magnitude of their number in glory. The other fact is that if they are children then of course they have not been "defiled;" and to make this expression refer to that is to accuse the Holy Ghost of uttering a preposterous and needless saying.

Our own firm belief is that the 144,000 stand for those who were sanctified in this life, waiting not for the dying hour to receive a work of grace which Christ stands ready and willing and able to perform at the present moment. When we remember what it costs to obtain this blessing—what ridicule, opposition, persecution, and ecclesiastical rejection it invariably entails—we are not surprised that the suffering ones have a distinction accorded them that is not granted to all who are in heaven.

We have made the point elsewhere that all believers must be sanctified before seeing the Lord, and that many obtain this grace only on a death-bed, because they heard not of it, or were not properly taught; or, as is most generally the case, were unwilling to pay the great cost of the experience.

The question may be raised, if all of us either in life or in the death hour obtain sanctification, why should there be a difference existing between us in heaven?

To this we reply that He who says that as " one star differeth from another star," so also shall be our resurrection body; and he who is to say to one, " Take thou authority over ten cities," and to another, " Rule thou over five cities," he is a just God and will do right. Moreover, let it be remembered that there is bound to be a great difference in the faith, life, religious character, labors, and sacrifices of a man, who sought the blessing of holiness at the cost of the death of self, the loss of all things, keeping it in face of raging devils, a hating world, a ridiculing and persecuting Church, and that man who obtains it in a dying hour. If any one thinks that such a life will not be accorded a special distinction in the world to come, he has forgotten that God is just; and

15

needs to be reminded that the Scripture itself
ends with a recognition of two grades of spiritual
life in heaven. Hear it: " He that is righteous,
let him be righteous still: and he that is holy, let
him be holy still."

Sanctification in death gives that purity or holiness of heart without which no man shall see the
Lord, but it does not make up for the life that
could have been spent in such union and communion with God and such toil for souls as would
have told on the world and Church forever. The
character is crystallized at death; the book is finished; the tree lies as it falls; we take rank in
heaven as we actually were in God's sight on
earth. A faith that recognized and took Christ
as the uttermost Saviour, as a Sanctifier as well
as Pardoner, was bound on earth to affect the
soul's life and development, and is bound for the
"blood's sake" to be honored and distinguished
in heaven. It is after all a distinction of grace.
Christ is honored by it.

With these thoughts in mind, let us see if we
can find any signs or features about the 144,000
that would confirm the assertion that they represent the sanctified.

One is that it is a much smaller band than the
other. The first cannot be numbered, but the

second is 144,000. This disparity has always been seen on earth, and it is not surprising that it should appear in heaven. For some reason comparatively few have accepted the grace of sanctification. In our Church membership, pastors report hundreds of regenerated members, but only a dozen or score of sanctified ones. In the revival it is often the same way: scores are pardoned, but only a few are purified. This is to be accounted for partly through lack of instruction of the people, and partly because it costs more to be sanctified than justified. To obtain the latter a man gives up his sins; to secure the former he gives up himself. Regeneration is a birth, while sanctification is a crucifixion. It is easier both in the physical and spiritual world to be born than to die. This explains why there is a great multitude in heaven which cannot be numbered, and right in the same heaven another company of one hundred and forty and four thousand.

Some objector may say that the 144,000 is a very small number to describe the sanctified hosts of all ages. But we must bear in mind that it is a symbolic figure, and does not mean literally 144,-000. On the other hand, it is not to be construed as meaning an innumerable host like the other, because the perfect number twelve is multiplied by another perfect number twelve, thereby producing the doubly perfect number 144. This mistake we are saved from making by observing that the 144,-000 is contrasted in size with the innumerable multitude. The whole truth taught is that while the 144,000 is a much smaller company than the innumerable multitude, it is nevertheless a perfect number.

A second fact appearing is that the 144,000 were all " sealed." This is not said of the innumerable multitude. Sealing cannot be birth. A thing has to be born or made before it can be sealed. So right here appears a second work of grace. This is made perfectly clear in Ephesians i. 13: " In whom ye also trusted, after that ye heard the word of truth, . . . in whom ALSO, AFTER THAT YE BELIEVED, YE WERE SEALED with that Holy Spirit of promise." The emphasized words clearly show that there is a subsequent work of grace that is here called sealing.

Webster says that to seal is to confirm, ratify, establish, to make fast, to keep secure or secret. None of these terms can be twisted into synonyms of the word " regeneration."

History teaches us that when the Roman Governor had sealed the tomb of our Lord it meant that no one could enter. It was made inviolable. The Roman Government stood by and behind that seal.

Daily life tells us that when one seals an envelope from that moment something is shut up for himself and another. It means secrecy, sacredness, and peculiar ownership. The letter is first written and then sometime after sealed. So God writes his law and deposits his love in our hearts. He places very precious things there. Afterward he seals. There is a second work of grace that brings the soul into a sacred nearness to God, into a hidden and, to outsiders, a mysterious life. There is a holy grace that shuts one up and in with God. There is a delightful understanding, a blessed secret between the sealer and the sealed, known only to them.

God's peculiar protection and ownership is seen, and, above all, deliciously felt in the seal. Who dares to tamper with a sealed letter or package? Whereas, an open missile or bundle is a temptation and invitation to prying eyes and ruthless fingers.

The soul instinctively craves this second and finishing work of God. The Methodist Church acknowledges the fact in one of its celebrated hymns, where, after a lament over wandering, there is immediately added a petition:

> Here's my heart, O take and SEAL it,
> Seal it for thy courts above.

According to this hymn the " sealing " comes afterward. St. Paul declares the same thing: "In whom also, AFTER that ye believed, ye were sealed."

A third fact stated is that they were taken from Israel—some from Judah, Simeon, and the other tribes, but all from Israel. This is deeply significant. It shows that the smaller band came out of the great multitude; that the sanctified are found in and lifted from the regenerated, or God's Israel.

A fourth feature of the 144,000 is God's name in their foreheads. This is still more striking. It declares a higher grade of religious experience. It proclaims a manifest and unmistakable piety. What they were was evident to all. Their relation to God was the prominent and conspicuous fact of their lives. Certainly it is well for the cause of God when his people are thus easily recognized. It is not the case with all of his children, but it is invariably so with those who are genuinely sanctified. It is worthy of remark that the severe judgments and criticisms passed upon holiness people are in reference to their religious lives. No one accuses them of worldliness. As in the case of Daniel, the accusation is made about their worship, their self-denials, and their God. Their up-rightness is the prominent thing with them, it shines from their faces, it is written on their fore-heads. And the religious life is attacked because conspicuous.

A fifth feature noticeable is their joyous and fresh experience. The passage under scrutiny says that they sung, and it was a new song. Two things have invariably impressed us about the holi-ness people; one, their gladness, and the other the constant newness and freshness of their religious life and experience. As a holy man once said in our hearing, "every day is like a new conversion to my soul." They are the happiest people in the world to-day, always singing, shouting, or prais-ing God, and always having new and delight-ful manifestations of divine grace. Strike them where and when you will, they have just found something wonderfully precious in the Bible, or Christ has revealed himself in a blessed way to the heart, or in a marvelous manner in his provi-dence, and they are running over. They have the melody in the heart that Paul speaks of, and the "well of water" in the soul that Jesus told the Samaritan woman about: so who wonders at their gladness and spiritual freshness?

A sixth observable fact is that their experience

was a peculiar one. The third verse says that no
one could learn the song they sung but themselves.
So the innumerable multitude washed and saved
did not sing the song. Only the 144,000 could
sing it.

The teaching is unmistakable that there is a religious experience not known to all of God's children. It has always been so, and will be to the
end of time. Many could not sing the song that
the 144,000 sung. More than once the writer has
seen regenerated people try to imitate the sanctified in their experience and rejoicing, but it was
an evident and utter failure. The most difficult of
things to do is to praise God, and rejoice in spirit
and with lip when the spirit of praise and rejoicing is not in you. In the regenerated life this rejoicing comes at certain wide-apart times as a
result of much prayer, or revival effort. In the
sanctified life the inward rejoicing is a constant
experience, for the cause of it is indwelling and
abiding. How easy for them at all times to praise
God with this unfailing melody within, and salvation like a well of water gushing and springing up
in the soul all the time into everlasting life! while
how difficult and indeed impossible for those to do
so who are strangers to this work of grace! No
one could sing the song but the 144,000.

A seventh fact is their purity. They were not "defiled." Commentators like Dr. Clarke say this means simply spiritual chastity. Here are the pure in heart whom Christ in his sermon calls "blessed." There is a grace which keeps God's child unspotted from the world. There are such people to-day. They are a peculiar people; their garments are kept constantly white by the blood, and God continually abides in them and is glorified by them. They may be a small number compared to the great mass—perhaps as 144,000 to an innumerable multitude—but they exist for all that in this world, and will be signally rewarded in heaven.

An eighth description reveals the fact that there is no guile in their mouth.

If any one should ask me to name a distinguishing trait of sanctified people, I would reply that their conversation is in heaven, their language chaste and pure. No profane word repeated as having occurred in a story, no impure anecdote, nothing in the conversation that would show a relish for or bias of mind toward anything unclean. No slander nor abuse nor slang nor worldly fun nor low wit. The tongue is pure because the heart is clean. There is no guile in their mouth.

A ninth description shows them without fault before God; not without fault before men. There will never be a time that we will be able to measure up to the exacting standards of men. The Saviour himself could not please men, and brought upon himself their bitter censure. To the morally jaundiced eye of that period he was unlovely. But there is an experience where, in spite of adverse criticisms and disapproval in high places, you can still be without fault before God. Christ can do such a work in sanctification, that the heart is not only made pure, but kept pure, while the soul rejoices in an unbroken consciousness of divine approbation. The Bridegroom's affirmation to the soul married to him is: '' Thou art all fair, my love.''

A tenth description is that they '' followed the Lamb whithersoever he went.''

Here in a sentence we find that consecration, devotion, and perfect obedience that are the striking features of the life of holiness. The sanctified man is a follower of Christ in all things and at all times.

There are many Christians who will follow Christ, but not all the time and everywhere. Some things and places they shrink from. Some calls they do not heed, some crosses they will not take up. But the sanctified man is ready for Gethsemane with its loneliness, the judgment seat of man with its false witnessing, and the cross with its shame and suffering. All that is needed is for Christ to lead, and they will follow.

Does the reader see a difference between the two companies or not? A mightier faith, that claimed and received holiness in this life, results in a purer life and greater deeds for God. And the holy and just One who says "according to your faith" and according to the "deeds done in the body"—that Judge of perfect righteousness will honor the splendid royal faith that honors fully the blood, and there will be two companies as shown in Revelation. One believed in the power of the blood to pardon; the other, in its power to sanctify. One believed it could save us in sin; the other, that it could save us "from sin." One looked for perfect salvation in the future, at death, or in heaven; the other trusted for and obtained the full and perfect salvation as a present experience — now. Such a superior faith in Christ is bound to result in a more exalted experience and devoted life, and is compelled by a just God to be peculiarly honored in heaven.

Once admit what John insists on here—that there are two companies in heaven, no matter what has originated them—and the principle for which we contend is admitted. We cannot conceive of anything that could so properly account for the existence of the two bands, as the two differing faiths just mentioned, in the power of Christ's blood.

The innumerable company believed in it for pardon; the smaller company trusted it for holiness. The first looked for purity of heart to come in the future with the help of time and growth in grace; the second, trusting in the blood alone, believed for and accepted sanctification now.

It is this second and smaller company that most honored Christ: and it is not surprising that he should be seen peculiarly honoring them in the day of rewards and in the kingdom of heaven.

CHAPTER XXX.

IT was a long time before the writer could realize that the soul was granted two relations to God before entering upon eternity. This tardy discovery seems strange when we have many figurative teachings in the Bible covering this truth, and other passages that plainly declare it to be a fact. When we see in the Old Testament the bond servant and love slave, and hear Christ in the gospel speaking of servants and friends, this of itself should prepare us for the acceptance of the thought of two distinct experiences of grace.

Concerning the relation of sonship to God there is no doubt in the Church to-day. The fact is stated in the word that through regeneration or the new birth we become the sons of God. " The Spirit itself beareth witness with our spirits that we are the children of God." He has sent forth the spirit of his Son in our hearts, teaching us to cry: Abba Father. Right here most Christians stop, and suppose there is nothing more possible for the soul, except to become more faithful and devoted as the children of heaven.

There is, however, another and nearer relation that the soul can enjoy toward the Lord, that is embodied in the word and figure of marriage.

Reason itself approves the idea, even if it could not in the first instance have suggested it. One day the writer was near a minister of the gospel who was kneeling at the altar. He was saying that he felt he was God's son and realized his acceptance, and could not think of anything better to be enjoyed than what he now possessed. Our reply was: " Can you conceive of a relation nearer to you than that of your child? Is there not some one who is closer to you than your son? Can any one get nearer to you than your wife?" At once his eyes filled with tears and he bowed his head on the altar in silence. We saw that he grasped the gracious design of God, and were gladdened to see him soon after receive the blessing.

The Bible to the anointed eye is very clear in its teaching of this relationship. Ezekiel in the sixteenth chapter of his prophecy has a most exquisite picture concerning it. The Song of Solomon is devoted altogether to the idea. Again it appears in the Epistle to the Ephesians, where the Church is represented by Paul in that tender and beautiful light. Still again in Revelation Christ is described as a bridegroom coming for his bride, who has made herself ready. And the Saviour himself teaches it in his parable of the wise and foolish virgins. Many interpreters of the parable have made the profound mistake of supposing that everybody is going to fall into spiritual sleep before Christ's coming, because both wise and foolish virgins are seen slumbering before the arrival of the bridegroom; when the fact is that the sanctified Church which never slept is represented not by the virgins, but by the invisible and unmentioned Bride of the parable, who, the reader may be sure, never closed her eyes. The idea of a bride sleeping when the bridegroom is on the way to her to have the nuptials celebrated! The attendants may sleep over some delay, but not the bride.

The question may be asked in what respect is this second relation superior to the first, or that of sonship?

One answer is that it is the most intimate of relations. A friend is near, but the wife is nearer. A business partner knows many secrets, but the wife possesses the whole heart. The child has many confidences reposed in its keeping, but the wife is still ahead. So is the union of the soul with Christ. It is so intimate that the Saviour says that he declares all to it that he has heard from the Father. The Bible teaches that in the true marriage two become one. Duality is lost in unity. Who can or should come in between husband and wife? This wonderful intimacy God uses to describe the state existing between himself and the sanctified soul.

Furthermore, it is the most tender of relations. Let the reader turn to the passage in Scripture where it is said that as a bridegroom rejoiceth over his bride so does the Lord over us. It is easy to tell a bridal couple in traveling. It is equally easy to tell when the soul has been wedded to Christ. The holy endearments, the silent raptures of love that are realized in that experience can only be known to those that have entered the state.

It is the most satisfying of relations. Men and women were made to be mated. Until that is consummated, a sense of incompleteness is felt. It is declared in many a fit of inward restlessness, and exhibited in external ways as well. But how they settle down when marriage takes place! Now begins the rest-life indeed. The writer has noticed travelers arriving at the depot, hurrying off at once to the spot called home, where waited the woman whom they had selected above all others to be the friend, companion, and partner of life.

They had no desire to linger on the street. The loadstone was yonder. The satisfying life had been found in the married estate and home life.

Regeneration does much for the soul, but one thing is certain: it has not satisfied and rested it according to its cravings. The longing is still there. There is a cry for another blessing. There is a yearning to know and enjoy Christ as never before. The soul wants to settle down and rest, with the Saviour as its husband and its home in God. This is found alone in sanctification. From that moment the heart could voice its profound content in the words: " I am at home, at rest, and satisfied." The soul is at home, and with One who is the Chief among ten thousand. How little does it care in its wedded joys for the things outside that men value and emphasize! Happiness and restfulness have been found in the spirit's marriage to Christ. It now rests at his feet, hears his voice, feels his glance of love, and is satisfied.

Again, it is a life of utter absence of care. It is not difficult to tell the woman who has to struggle for bread and shield herself and children, and the woman whose husband is living and able to provide and protect. The first has an anxious and careworn look; the second is the picture of

16

rest. One is planning and laboring as a bread-winner; the other is simply a housekeeper, while the husband keeps his eye on wood pile and flour barrel, and renews with regular hand every want and waste of the family.

When the soul becomes satisfied, or married to Christ, the old-time care ends. A conscious provider is in the life. The bread question is settled. All questions affecting self and welfare and future movements are settled. The feeling is that Christ is going to take care of soul and body, meet every emergency, provide for every want, deliver from every foe, and be with us and in us forever.

It is a life of growing likeness to each other. All of us have noticed this at times in regard to married people; that where the marriage is indeed of God they manifest increased resemblance to each other as the years pass by. We know not the law that produces the strange result, but cannot but observe the fact. In the spiritual life we see the same transformation taking place, and that the sanctified person becomes daily more and more like the Saviour. The light deepens in the countenance, the manner becomes tenderer, and the whole spirit, bearing, and appearance more and more like Christ. You cannot look on some sanctified faces without thinking of Christ.

It is a life of increasing knowledge and understanding of each other. Let the reader study two people who have been wedded a long time. The daily contact with each other for years has taught them a thorough mutual understanding. It is delightful to see how they anticipate each other's wants and know how to please one another. A peculiar language, not of words, seems to have sprung up between them. The right thing is done often without a word. They seem to know each other's minds without a sentence being spoken. Their lives fit into each other, and have become as one. This beautiful and mysterious understanding is seen in its full power in sanctification. The purified soul needs no thundering sermon to be directed aright. Such an one walks so close to God and has been so long with him that he is " guided by His eye." The slightest wave of Christ's hand, the gentlest movement of the Spirit is sufficient to lead, restrain, turn, or stop. The soul by long dwelling with Jesus has got to understand him and seems intuitively to know his will in all matters and to anticipate his every desire. The individual is where Paul placed him in the words, " hid with Christ." He is lost in God. The prayer of Christ in the seventeenth chapter of John is answered, and the soul has become " one in us " " as thou, Father, art in me, and I in thee."

Of course this thorough understanding does not come at once. The young wife is not able, though willing, to do what years alone will teach her. The blessing of sanctification is purity, but maturity comes with the sweep of years. It is the intimate living with the Lord, seen in the sanctified experience, that occasions this perfect adaptation and beautifully harmonious life with God that is so mighty in its effects upon the observant world.

It is a lifelong partnership. The child comes and goes, the daughter marries and resides in a distant State, the son leaves the paternal mansion and goes off to marry and battle in life for himself; but the wife stays.

There is an abidingness, if I may be allowed to coin a word, a stay-at-home quality in the sanctified soul that is pleasing to God and blessed to the soul itself. As marriage is for life, so sanctification takes the Lord for all time. As a woman, when married and escorted to her home, enters with a feeling that she is rightfully, restfully, and permanently there, and so acts; so the soul, in this blessed experience, enters upon a confiding, hiding, and abiding life in Christ that is beyond

words to describe. It feels at home, it has come
to stay, it has consummated an eternal partnership with one who does not believe in divorce.

It is interesting to see how we can enter upon
this experience. And here the figure itself held
up in the. Word of God and dwelt upon in this
chapter gives the answer.

First, there is a divine wooing. In the Song of
Solomon Christ is represented as seeking the
Church, then withdraws himself and she follows
him. In our social life the wooer comes and departs, and by and by is followed by the yearning
heart of the woman visited. In the spiritual life
Christ visits us and wooes us for the higher blessing, symbolized by marriage. Every regenerated
person with an experience worth mentioning has
felt coming into his life the call of Christ to
something higher and better. Then occur the
withdrawals; and then should be seen at once in
us what is noticed in the Church as described in
the Song: we should arise and seek the with-
drawn Christ.

Secondly, there must be a preference for Christ
above all others. This is a necessary step in se-
curing an earthly marriage, and is certainly essential in the spiritual life. Fame may be beckoning,
Ambition whispering at the ear, Wealth pouring

its treasures at the feet, Pleasure may smile, and the World promise you great things; but turning from them all, you must prefer Christ. The soul must say: "He is the Chief among ten thousand to me; he is altogether lovely."

Thirdly, there must be an act of surrender. We have known of instances where the woman loved an individual above all others, but would not give herself in marriage to him. This surrender is bound to precede the nuptials. When analyzed, it amounts to this.

The hand is bestowed on the suitor. So is the hand given to Christ to write, work, give, or do anything for him.

The whole heart is likewise given. No true man would marry where this is not done. And certainly Christ will never sanctify the soul unless the undivided heart has been yielded to him. Let the reader observe that pardon or justification cannot be typified in this figure, for a sinner has no love to give.

The name is given up. The fact of a woman surrendering her name for another is a touching sign of one life becoming merged in another. She gives up her name and takes his, no matter what that name is and may bring. So in sanctification a man yields his name. It can now be dealt with by the world as it wills. He ceases defending it and writing about it. He has changed it for another.

Self is given up. What a gift that is! We marvel that a man can ever be anything but tender to a woman who has thus presented herself to him. In like manner we present ourselves to Christ. In the words of Inskip we say: "I am, O Lord, wholly and forever thine." Need we marvel after this at Christ's tenderness with the sanctified?

The woman accepts the lot and future of her husband. On the marriage day everybody is left behind, no matter how dear; and she goes out alone into the world with the man of her choice. Good-bye to father, mother, brother, sister, friends, and everybody; farewell to house, yard, trees, hills, meadow, and the singing brook flowing by the home of her childhood. Now for new scenes with the man to whom she has given herself. His lot is hers henceforth. It may be a hard one, but it is hers. The husband may lead her forth to suffering and poverty; but she accepted all these possibilities in taking him, and goes out prepared for anything and everything. In like manner the soul wedded to Christ gives up all for him; father, mother, lands, friends, and fortune are forsaken.

The soul knows that Christ is unpopular with many, and will be rejected by great numbers; that there is still no room for him in the inn; that the synagogue continues to put him out, and the temple to stone him. But the soul is ravished with him, and prefers hardship, sorrow, and persecution with him rather than ease and earthly favor without him. The writer knew a young woman who left her husband to languish in sickness while she returned home; and another who went back to her father while she allowed her husband to struggle alone in the midst of desperate trials. But he knows many others who never would have done these things. The true wife stands by the lonely and struggling husband. And so the soul, in being wedded to Christ, takes him for good report or evil report, for richer or poorer, for better or for worse. Its constant cry is: " Take the world, take all, take everything; but give me Jesus."

CHAPTER XXXI.

IN a number of places through the Scriptures man is represented as being God's house. "Ye are God's building," it is said in one place, and again, "Ye are the temples of the Holy Ghost." In still another place God himself asks the question of his people as to the kind of house they would build him. The idea brought forward in the passage is that if heaven is his throne and the earth his footstool, what kind of a house would they think worthy of him? The thought is magnificent and overwhelming. The architectural pride of man is prostrated with the simple sentence. What indeed could be built out of wood and stone that would be the fitting temple of a Being inhabiting immensity? How inclose such a God in walls? How build at all, when all the wood and stone are but parts of God's footstool?

Strange to say that just at this moment when the greatness of the Almighty is thus brought forward, and man's inability to build worthy of him is seen, the Lord suddenly declares: "I dwell in the high and holy place, with him also that is of a

contrite and humble spirit." Refusing to abide
in houses of man's workmanship, yet he will dwell
in a human frame or tabernacle, which is the
work of his own hands.

God's plan thus announced becomes plainer
throughout the pages of Holy Writ.   He not only is
to " inhabit the praises of Israel," but will dwell in
the people themselves.   We have not time to trace
this thought as it is unfolded in the Word, but
point to its consummation on earth in the words of
Paul, " Christ in you the hope of glory," and the
blessed vision of heaven, where God is seen taber-
nacling with men, and in them forevermore.

Man then was made of God for the blessed purpose of dwelling in him.   This is far better than
standing in one's own righteousness.   Herein may
be seen the blessed provision against any future
fall, while at the same time it appears as an act of
love unsatisfied to be without, and only content to
be within the being made.   Love cannot endure
distance.

We are God's houses.   And such houses!   Did
ever house have such windows as those through
which the soul looks out on earth and sky?   Did
ever house have such a door as that from which
comes trooping such forms of beauty, wisdom,
eloquence, and song, clothed in variegated gar-

ments called speech or language, that the world
never wearies in looking upon, listening to, and
admiring them? And think also of a walking
house, a dwelling that can transport itself about,
and one of these days is to have wings. David,
giving a glance at the exterior of this marvelous
creation, said it was fearfully and wonderfully
made. And men of science, after studying for ages
its three stories, physical, intellectual, and spiritual,
look up and repeat the words of inspiration: "Man
is fearfully and wonderfully made."

To this house, made by the hand of God, stolen
and preëmpted by the devil, and now purchased
by the precious blood of Christ, to this house the
Saviour comes knocking and asking for admittance.

After repeated knocks, long waiting, and the
touching call "Behold, I stand at the door," at
last that door is opened, and Jesus, the true Owner, is admitted and welcomed.

We need not dwell upon the gladness of the
days that follow. The authority of Satan is at an
end, the house is now governed by the Holy One,
and is acknowledged and recognized to be the
property and home of Christ. Here is beheld regeneration, which as an experience is felt to be a
succession of visits from the Lord.

In making this statement we are upheld by the

experience of men and the teachings of the word
of God.   What converted man or woman on earth
but has to deplore again and again the absence of
Christ from the soul?   There may be no consciousness of sin, no backsliding, no renouncing
of his authority, no going back to the world; and
yet the delightful presence of the Saviour is
missed.   His smile has vanished, his voice is not
heard in the chambers of the heart, and in a word
he is absent.   What says the hymn

> How tedious and tasteless the hours
> When Jesus no longer I see?

The experiences of the regenerated in all ages
agree here, that at times, without any cause or
reason that they could see, Christ withdraws the
consciousness of his presence from the soul.

In the Bible this remarkable and peculiar fact is
unquestionably recognized.   In the Old Testament
God says to his people that he was as a traveler or
sojourner tarrying with them for a night, and then
gone again in the morning.   In the New Testament we have the sudden comings and goings of
the forty days, the drawing near on the highway,
and the unexpected vanishing from the supper
table at Emmaus.   Even in Revelation the promise to the man who will open the door is only to
sup with him, and not to abide.   Abiding is a dis-

tinct grace and experience. So we see that experience and the word agree.

Sanctification is the abiding or indwelling of Christ in the soul. There is a great difference between visiting a house and moving in to remain. The writer recalls delightful visitors to his childhood's home, who so charmed him that his great desire was that they would at once move in and live there all the time. He remembers distinctly the difference between the visits of a beautiful young lady and an agreeable young man and their coming at last to live with the family, the first marrying a brother and the second a sister of the writer. The visits were highly prized and fondly looked for, but the change of these charming people into household fixtures, so to speak, or into members and parts of the family and home life was something so much better every way that the horizon of a certain boy's life was wonderfully enlarged and filled from that day, and his happiness correspondingly increased.

Sanctification is the Lord coming in to abide in his house. The visiting is at an end, and the everlasting indwelling begins. If the reader desires to know whether the Bible bears us out in such an assertion, let him turn to the fourteenth chapter of John and in the sixteenth and seventeenth verses read as follows: " I will pray the Father, and he shall give you another Comforter, that he may *abide* with you forever; even the Spirit of truth; whom the world cannot receive, because it seeth him not, neither knoweth him: but ye know him; for he dwelleth with you, AND SHALL BE IN YOU."

Here is a promise made to disciples. In one verse the remarkable statement is made that He who has been dwelling *with* shall be *in* them, and in the other verse this new relation is said to be an " abiding forever."

In the twenty-third verse we have these additional words: " Jesus answered and said unto him, If a man love me, he will keep my words: and my Father will love him, and we will come unto him, and make our abode with him." Here the same thought is repeated. The condition is laid down of loving and obeying Christ, and when this is done the promise is that the Father and Son will take up their abode with us. When a person takes up his abode with another, it means that he comes into his house and stays there in a permanent fashion.

This is the gracious promise of the Saviour to his followers in the New Testament times as well as now. It was foreshadowed in the Temple, where the shekinah was seen dwelling in the Most Holy Place. The idea was kept up by frequent allusion to the fact of man's being the temple of the Lord, and was fulfilled on the day of Pentecost, when, according to the words of Christ in the fourteenth chapter of John, the Father, Son, and Spirit entered the disciples to abide with them forever.

The statements and teachings of the word are verified by experience. Thank God there are many in the land to-day, and the number is increasing, who know that Christ has something better for the soul than visits, no matter how frequent these visits may be. They have an experience in which there are no more comings and goings, appearances and disappearances, but the blessed, constant abiding presence of the Saviour. He has come to depart no more forever. He has come to stay. The visitor has become the indweller.

For over four years the writer has never lost consciousness of the presence of Christ. He knows of others who have enjoyed this grace for ten, fifteen, and twenty years, and still another who for half a century has never had the joy of the divine communion to cease nor the glory of that presence to be lifted.

Several things are observable in taking possession of a house. One is that it must be emptied.
The man who has purchased the property, before moving requires at the outset that it be emptied of the peculiar possessions of the one who
occupied it formerly. They may look very well,
but he does not desire them nor need them. Let
all go, the furniture in the room, the litter in the
garret, and the rubbish in the back yard.

In like manner an emptying of self is demanded
before Christ will take possession of our three-
story house of mind, soul, and body.

Another feature is the cleansing of the house.
Let the floors be cleansed, the windows washed,
walls wiped down, and yard swept up. No one
cares to move into an untidy dwelling. So there is a
cleansing required of us before God will enter to
stay. There is a sanctifying of self which precedes the sanctification wrought by the power of
God. St. Paul exhorted a Christian church to
" cleanse themselves from all filthiness of the flesh
and spirit " before they could perfect holiness in
the fear of God. Joshua bade the children of Israel to sanctify themselves before entering Caanan,
where God would acknowledge them as his holy
people before the heathen in the land.

Certainly if people will clean the house and yard

at the coming of an earthly friend, much more should they prepare for the coming into their lives of the Holy One of heaven.

It is at this point that stirring scenes take place. One day all the neighbors saw rolling up to the emptied and cleansed house a number of wagons and vans loaded with furniture, carpets, mirrors, pictures, and musical instruments; and then above all came the owner, who entered and took possession.

So happens it in grace, and all see it. To the emptied and cleansed life behold the Lord comes, in the presence of earth and heaven to take possession of his own. Chariots of fire bring the heavenly furniture. The candlestick of gold, the ark with its holy treasures, the bending angels, the drapery of love, the scarlet hangings of Calvary, the flashing mirror of the word, the golden harp, the white linen of the saints, and all the other beautiful treasures of the spiritual life.

But above all the Lord comes in himself. And this is the crowning joy and glory of it all: the Saviour has entered, and entered to abide forever.

The Master is in his house at last. After years of being shut out altogether, and years more of being received as a visitor, the Lord is now welcomed as being the undisputed owner and ever-

17

lasting indweller of a house doubly his by creation and redemption.

The writer in other years has seen a noble-looking mansion sitting dark and solitary in a grove of sighing trees. The owner and his family were in some distant city or State living there for months or years at a time, and so the home was left with forsaken grounds, grass-grown walks, closed doors, and darkened windows. The heart would feel a sensation of pain whenever the eyes would rest upon the scene. A visit now and then from the family or part of the family was like a sunburst on a cloudy day. But they would be off again in a few hours or days, and the house and grounds would take upon themselves the former lonely and sorrowful appearance.

One evening as people passed in the dusk they saw the house all lighted up. There was life and animation everywhere. Light streamed from the hall way and twinkled and glanced in the windows. Forms were seen flitting to and fro in the building. The laugh of servants in the yard, the prattle of children in the porch, and the voice of singing from the library floated out upon the night air. Warmth, light, color, movement, and gladness were seen everywhere. The owner had come home. It was not a visit to last a few days and then leave the home plunged again in loneliness and darkness; but he had come this time to remain, and the bright, animated scene before the eyes was the result.

So have we seen a life, gloomy, desolate, and forbidding. The windows of the soul were darkened, the door of the mouth was locked, the daughters of song and praise were still, and not a light shone from the face. It was evident that the Master of the house was absent.

Then came the time that Christ was admitted and beholders were made to rejoice over the signs of life and gladness which immediately appeared. But the joy and animation were not permanent. There would be lapses again and again into silence and gloom. The Lord's house suddenly became dark and quiet and would present the mournful appearance of being forsaken again. The Master was not to be seen, and the house sat in shadow and solitariness.

But the man was seen again, and this time the Lord had come to stay. And what a transformation? Fires burned on the hearthstone of the heart, lights streamed from the soul windows, forms of strength and beauty were seen flitting through the house or standing at the door, sounds of holy singing and happy laughter floated out on the air, and warmth and color, bustle and activity were seen everyhere about the divinely filled and furnished house.

And the last state was permanent. See the man where and when you will, and he is the same. The light in the face, the warmth in the soul, the song in the heart, and the joyous laugh and praise of the lip are fixed features and conditions. The constant, abiding presence of the Lord Jesus is the explanation. The Divine Visitor has become the Indweller.

CHAPTER XXXII.

CIRCUMCISION.

FOR the source of the thoughts that appear in this chapter the reader is referred to Deuteronomy xxx. 6: "And the Lord thy God will circumcise thine heart, . . . to love the Lord thy God with all thy heart, and with all thy soul, that thou mayest live."

There is no need to dwell upon the history of the rite of circumcision. Suffice it that it was observed by the children of Israel at the command of God.

By reference to Romans ii. 29 we discover that Paul spiritualized the rite and made it to stand for a work of grace that could not possibly be regeneration. By turning to Wesley's sermons it will be found that he has one on the circumcision of the heart, which he identifies with sanctification.

Here are Moses, Paul, and Wesley, all agreed in regard to the spiritual meaning of this carnal rite. Some people protest against spiritualizing any Scripture. We refer these objectors to the author and book of Hebrews. In this epistle Paul spiritualizes the priestly office, the wanderings of the Israelites, the crossing of the River Jordan, Melchizedec, the covenants, the tabernacle, and a number of other things.

We are well aware that this verse in Deuteronomy has been quoted by many to describe regeneration: but like other passages similarly claimed, it has been incorrectly used. There is not in the verse any allusion whatever to regeneration.

A second work of grace subsequent to regeneration is plainly taught by the very figure itself of circumcision.

Let it be remembered that regeneration is represented in the Bible under the figure of birth. Hence Christ says, "Ye must be born again;" and Paul speaks of our being the children of God, through the power of regeneration. Now if God wishes us to understand his Word, he will not use another figure to describe regeneration that plainly clashes with the first. If he did, who could possibly interpret the meaning of the Bible, and what confusion would be wrought!

Alas that this confusion has been produced by expositors of the Scripture who have claimed for regeneration what God has never affirmed was in it; have quoted passages that refer only to sanctification as proving the doctrine of regeneration; and have thus been under the necessity of accepting figures of speech and forms of illustration that clearly contradict each other and make the Almighty to have uttered folly!

No passage has been oftener quoted to prove regeneration than Deuteronomy xxx. 6, in which is stated: " The Lord thy God will circumcise thine heart, . . . to love the Lord thy God with all thine heart, and with all thy soul, that thou mayest live."

Let the reader with an unprejudiced mind take note of the following thoughts we offer, and see that the verse does not and cannot refer to regeneration, but to the work of sanctification.

One fact we call attention to is that circumcision always *follows* birth. A child had to be born before the rite of circumcision could be administered. Life, breath, voice, motion invariably preceded what is spoken of in the text. Not only that, but nourishment, so that the child grew and strengthened before it was circumcised. Indeed, God, in order to distinguish the two facts and their spiritual application to experiences in the kingdom of grace, separated them by a dash or interval of eight days. This being so, God will respect his own figures and imagery, and will not compare regeneration to birth in one place and to circumcision in another. Knowing as we do that the latter must of necessity follow the former in the physical kingdom, we feel that a truthful interpretation of the text in question reveals a second work of grace subsequent to spiritual birth or regeneration.

And this is just what sanctification is in our experience. It follows regeneration. We had life, breath, motion, nourishment, and growth before we received it. Mr. Wesley says he never knew of a case where a man secured both works at the same moment. And while we have heard of several, and have seen two who claimed to have been made marvelously to differ from all other creatures in that they really received both blessings at the same moment; yet upon inquiry of themselves a religious childhood has been made to appear, which they had counted for nothing, and in receiving sanctification afterward mistook the grace and called it regeneration.

We note a second fact: that circumcision is an excision. Again remember that regeneration is a birth, and that a creature has to be born before you can take anything from him. The child unborn may have a curious formation or excrescence upon the body, but birth must take place first, and the surgical operation will be attended to later.

Vain is the rebutting sarcasm flung at us " that

a hen never lays a rotten egg." The witty divine that perpetrated this needs to be reminded that the laying of an egg is not birth, but that takes place properly in hatching. Moreover, his argument recoils on himself in another way; for if we grant that the laying of an egg stands for birth, then still is there seen another work necessary before the chicken is beheld. It should be remembered, however, that regeneration is not likened to egg laying, but to birth as seen in the physical world, which allows the thought of a subsequent excision. Let it also be borne in mind that regeneration adds something, but the work mentioned in the verse under examination is that of substraction or removal.

A third fact drawn from this passage of Scripture is that love for God already existed before the work spoken of takes place. Let the reader mark that it does not say that the heart is circumcised in order that we should love God. If any one had questioned the writer's love for God in his regeneration, he could have easily disproved it in heart and in life. He knew well the moment when the sweet unearthly affection was implanted in' him by the divine hand. For fourteen years it was the controlling principle of his life. Love for God comes at the new birth, causing the soul to cry out in truth: "Abba, Father."

A fourth fact appearing is that this circumcision takes place that we should love the Lord with *all* the heart and *all* the soul. This agrees exactly with the experience of regenerated people. They love God, but they find idols within, things that dispute God's supreme reign, objects that divide the affections with him in an alarming way, a something inside that antagonizes the love of God and keeps the man from saying, as he longs to do, "I love God with all my heart." Sanctification, which is spiritual circumcision, takes out that indwelling something, and the soul to its delight discovers a perfect love to God at all times.

It is in full harmony with this idea that in the Discipline of our Church all preachers knocking for admittance into the Conference are asked not if they love God, but if they are groaning after perfect love; not growing, but *groaning;* not if they expect to be developed into it, but *made* perfect in love.

A fifth teaching of the passage is that this subsequent grace is the work of God. The verse says: "The Lord thy God will circumcise thine heart." How this single scripture, when studied and properly understood, annihilates the heresies in the Church to-day in regard to sanctification!

The Lord will do it; not time, not growth, not

Christian work. These three are all false saviors, and are utterly unable to remove from within us that dark, sad, troublesome something which hinders the regenerated man's love, faith, and rest from being perfect. The Lord will do it, and he alone can do it, and blessed be his name, he does it.

It is a curious and confirmatory fact that all who look to time, growth in grace, and Christian activity never get rid of that heavy, sorrowful something within the soul, which many in the Church to-day seem loath to name and to admit is in them. But all who come to the Lord and wait on him in the divinely appointed way get to see the Saviour in a new light, feel his power in a new way, and have a second blessing to talk about all the rest of their days.

A sixth lesson taught by this wonderful verse is that this subsequent work of heart circumcision is instantaneous. How long did it take the Jewish priest to administer the rite of circumcision? The preparation might have required minutes or hours, but circumcision itself was the occurrence of a second. So with sanctification; there may be indeed a gradual approach to it, a slow yielding of the will to the acceptance of the grace, but the work itself is instantaneous.

When Mr. Wesley said that sanctification is both gradual and instantaneous, he did not mean that some were sanctified gradually in contrast to others who received it immediately, but he was referring to the fact that there is a gradual yielding or approach of the man to the point or place where God instantaneously sanctifies him. There is always a cleansing or sanctifying of self requiring generally some minutes or hours of time before God performs his immediate sanctifying work. Sanctification proper, like regeneration, cannot be anything else but instantaneous. The same embarrassment which confronts us with the idea of a gradual regeneration, suggesting the inquiry as to what part of the soul is first converted, meets us at the bare hint of a gradual sanctification. As in the case just mentioned, we might well ask what part of the soul and life is first made holy.

There is a growth in grace that precedes and follows sanctification, but the last-named work, which means the removal of inbred sin and the entrance of the Lord as a perpetual abider in the soul, must and does take place instantly. The will of God, long ago expressed, prepares us to believe this. The power of God reveals how it is to be done. The aorist tense in which the verb appears when the Bible speaks of this work, a tense always signifying an immediate work, is additional proof; and the witnesses filling the land to-day by thousands and tens of thousands declaring that they all received it in a single moment of time, places the matter beyond peradventure.

The seventh fact stated by the passage is that when the work of circumcision is performed in the heart the man then lives. This certainly does not mean that there had been no life before in the regenerated heart, for regeneration is the implantation of spiritual life. But as we have known it said by one party to another, " If you want to live, come to our country," the reference being to superior advantages and enjoyments, so here the promise in the text directs the mind to a grace and experience so real and blessed and superior that it is likened to life itself.

The regenerated man lives, it is true, but he is conscious of faintings of heart, swoonings of energy, coldness of spirit, and a " body of death " in him that both distresses and alarms. If we saw a man in our midst given to fainting spells, sudden fits of unconsciousness, profound prostrations now and then with all the appearance of death upon him, we would hardly feel that he was entitled to all the richness and force that is found

in the word " life." We would say to the man,
come to such a place, and do this and that, and
you will know what *life* is.

In the regenerated life a man knows a fluctuating experience of strength and weakness, living
and dying. All converted people who are willing to admit the truth at the cost of what they
claim for regeneration say this is their experience.
Hundreds of them have personally confessed this
mournful fact to the writer. Even when they do
not yield to sin, they are conscious of a body
of death that is continually throwing out its chilling influence upon prayer, praise, testimony, and
life. This, taken with sudden faintings of spirit,
fits of lethargy, times of moral weakness, not to
say helplessness, prevents us from allowing to
them in the way of description all that is in the
word " life."

Hence it is that, taking up the Word of God, we
say: Let God circumcise your heart; let this inward disturbing cause, this body of death, be removed, and you will live. And it will be life indeed. It will be a life without the antagonism of
an inward spiritual disease. It will be life, not
only free, but full, abundant, and overflowing.
This is the very thing that was in the mind of the
Saviour when he said, talking about his sheep:

" I am come that they might have life, *and* that they might have it more abundantly." "And" is a copulative conjunction, and means something additional. The disciples had life previous to the baptism of the Holy Ghost, but after that took place on the morning of Pentecost, they had life " more abundantly." From that time they lived.

It is the full, overflowing, and abiding blessing which comes in sanctification, that makes a person feel when he obtains it that now he lives indeed. O for the circumcision of the hearts of God's people, that they might understand and experience all that is in the word " life," and be able to say: " I love God with all my heart and with my whole soul.

CHAPTER XXXIII.

CRUCIFIXION.

THERE are some verses and paragraphs in the Scripture that so clearly teach a higher life that the regenerated feels it to be a mockery to quote them as describing his state before God and daily experience. If a preacher, he finds a difficulty in handling them; and if he does present them in the pulpit, he realizes in the progress and conclusion of the sermon that he has not gotten at the heart of the text and revealed the holy things therein enshrined. Among a number of such passages is one in Galatians ii. 20: "I am crucified with Christ." The first glance shows that there is no ordinary experience, but an extraordinary one. Reflection convinces that the regenerated man cannot claim this as describing and covering his life. The fact is, it is one of Paul's testimonies to sanctification. The figure of the cross is used to describe the blessing. Who, indeed, but a sanctified man could say truthfully: "I am crucified with Christ?"

The figure teaches a second work of grace. Unquestionably a person must be born before he can be crucified. Regeneration, we know, is called a birth in the Word of God. But here in Galatians ii. 20 is a work and experience spoken of that is bound to be subsequent to birth; and if so, it proves the fact of a second work. We may be assured that God is not going to mix figures; and when he says that regeneration is birth, he certainly will not state elsewhere that it is a crucifixion. This would be to illustrate it with things antipodal and irreconcilable to each other, would confuse the Bible student, and convict the Almighty of folly. The teaching is that just as crucifixion follows birth, so sanctification, as an experience, follows regeneration.

This second work, as taught by the figure, is a divine work. That the crucifixion mentioned is of God is seen in the words: " God forbid that I should glory, save in the cross of our Lord Jesus Christ, by whom the world is crucified unto me, and I unto the world." So, then, it is Christ, or the cross of Christ (and they mean the same), which crucifies us to the world. Many feel the need of this crucifixion; but are looking to old age, time, and trouble to produce the state that should exist in the soul toward a God-hating and God-forgetting world. They are false saviors all. It is the Lord himself only who can do the deed. Here,

18

then, is an experience mentioned in Galatians that is not birth, but is compelled to follow birth, and the experience is credited to divine power. What other conclusion could we draw from it but that there are two works of grace for the soul?

A third truth taught by the figure is that of the loss sustained through the cross. The man condemned to be crucified went forth to the place of death with nothing on earth left him but the cross. In like manner, in spiritual crucifixion everything is given up. The world is left behind with all it possesses and offers: the good opinion of men, human favor and patronage, home and pleasing associations, personal ease and comfort; indeed, everything is left behind, as with the cross upon our shoulder we turn the face to Calvary to be crucified with Christ. All is gone but the cross. In fact, we have, by a close study, discovered the full beauty and glory of the cross, and pant for that alone. We are willing to give up everything for it. The light and attraction that formerly rested on things of sense and time have removed and settled on the cross of Christ. The heart has been undeceived in its quest for happiness. The sweet revelation made is that it is not to be found by avoiding the cross, or by taking up a part of it, or cutting off a portion, but by taking up the cross as a whole; and the yearning is not for a painted cross, or one bejeweled, or covered with flowers, but the old, plain, rugged, heavy cross of Christ. Strange to the on-looking world, but not to the seeker; the soul cries out for the cross, the whole cross, the old cross. The closer we get to the Saviour, the nearer we draw to the blessing of holiness; the more precious becomes the cross; and the more convinced we are that it is really what our panting, aching, restless hearts need. Feeling that it is the pearl of great price, we willingly sell all other pearls for it; convinced that it is the soul's happiness and highest good, we gladly suffer the loss of all things for its sake.

A fourth fact made to appear is the pain that is bound to be realized at this time. Crucifixion is not a pleasant death, but attended with unspeakable suffering. Let no one be deceived in regard to the pangs that precede sanctification. They are sharp and many. Nails are driven just where we are tenderest, and by the very hands we least expected. The vinegar will be offered in abundant measures, both in speech and manner. As we draw nigh the blessing that is to release us from this kind of suffering for evermore, gibes, wagging heads, pointing fingers, and derisive speeches will abound.

Many seek sanctification by easy routes. They
like the rocking-chair and good book way.   If the
cross must be endured, they have a way of slant-
ing it, so that they do not have to hang perpendic-
ularly, or on the straight up and down way demanded by the gospel. They somehow recline
on the cross so there is not much weight felt.
Sometimes cushions are provided to soften its exactions; and instead of nails through the palms,
ribbons and gum elastic bands around the wrist
are used.   The result is that some kind of blessing is obtained, a kind of popular holiness that is
about as soft and molluscous in its character as
the sacrifice itself that was made.

The figure of the cross used in the passage tells
us what to expect—namely, sharp, varied, and
protracted pains before the blessed end comes.

A fifth feature is loneliness.   A man going outside of the city walls to be crucified walks a lonely way.   No pleasing companionships appear at
such an hour, no friend is in sight, none of the
bystanders offer sympathy or offer to help bear
the cross; he goes out alone, hangs alone, and
dies alone.

He that seeks sanctification must expect loneliness.   He will be shunned by the crowd as soon
as his determination and destination is made to ap-

pear. The Sanhedrim will condemn, the priests will hold themselves aloof, the people will be partly bewildered and partly awed into silence at what is taking place, and even the daughters of Jerusalem, gazing with eyes of sympathy on the scene, will stand afar off.

Loneliness must be endured. It is necessary for the obtainment of the blessing. It is well to court solitude at this time. Seek not human presence and sympathy. Like Jacob, spend the entire night in prayer with God. Bear the solitariness that comes from being uplifted on the cross above the noisy, laughing, jeering crowd below. Christ was lonely for us; let us endure the solitary experience that precedes sanctification for his sake and our soul's sake.

A sixth feature is that of shame. We need not try to prove to the reader that crucifixion was an ignominious death. Does it not strike the mind with force that in holding up this blessing of holiness Paul should use the figure of the cross? The teaching is that it is and will ever be an experience of shame to the world.

It is interesting to try to locate the offense of the cross to-day. It certainly is not in the fact of Church membership, nor in the doctrine of the witness of the Spirit, nor in that of regeneration.

Where is it? Let the reader get right quiet and look around and listen. Upon what is the laughter and ridicule of men in and out of the Church being turned to-day? What is it to-day in the religious life that is felt to be a shame and reproach to confess? The answer is: Sanctification. Are we willing to bear the shame of the cross as the Lord once did? Paul says, " He suffered outside the gate " " that he might sanctify the people," and adds, " Let us go forth therefore unto him without the camp, bearing his reproach." So that is the reproach. Will we bear it?

Christians sing: " Where he leads me I will follow." He leads us up on the cross. Will we follow him, or do we prefer to go on singing falsehoods? There he hangs on the cross. How the crowd pointed the finger, jeered, and laughed at him! Reader, are you willing to go up where he is? Will you say, " Now, Lord, let me come; I want to be with you," and then nestle down in the place where he has been waiting for you so long?

A seventh feature is that of the dying on the cross. There is an unmistakable experience of the dying of self to this world before the blessing of sanctification rushes like a new life upon the soul. There is a consciousness of dying to all things, to human favor, human fear, and to the world itself. How the earth fades away to the sight and becomes of trifling moment to the mind and heart of one who is being crucified with Christ.

Just as a man dying physically bestows his money, property, and valuables upon his children and friends who stand around, saying, " You can have this, and you can take that; I want them no longer; I am leaving them forever," so the soul approaches the death of self; surrenders the things to others that he once held dear; and leaves popularity, fame, personal comfort, and all else to those who love and want them. They have lost their charm to his dying gaze and their power over his heart. He turns from them wearily, as an expiring man does on his bed, and fixes his glance and attention on other and better and everlasting things. Here we see the crucifixion feature of sanctification, where as yet God's hand of power has not been signally and consciously manifested. Much of what has been described has to be done by the man himself, and are experiences that invariably precede the divine work of sanctification.

Here is the gradual work that Mr. Wesley mentions in speaking of the blessing of holiness.

When he said that sanctification was both gradual
and instantaneous, he did not mean that some
people obtain the experience gradually, in contrast to others who receive the grace instantaneously; but he simply meant that there was a gradual
work and progress upon the part of man, assisted
by divine grace, that preceded an instantaneous
work that is wrought by the Lord alone. In other
words, there is a crucifying before there is a crucifixion; there is dying before death.

The last truth suggested by the figure is the
death itself that takes place upon the cross. Just
as the moment comes to one hanging on the cross
when the last breath is drawn, the head drops
upon the breast, and the man is dead. So there
is an instant when the struggles and sufferings of
the soul seeking sanctification cease, and the long-
looked-for death takes place. Inbred sin dies.
God kills that something within the Christian
breast that so burdened and troubled him. The
unmistakable feeling is that it is death.

There is a death to the world. Something happens in sanctification that causes the sanctified to
turn the eye of a dead man on the world. We
can conceive of a woman bepainted, bedizened,
and bejeweled, sporting herself before the glazed
eyes of a corpse; or a man with a sword or

cudgel trying to awaken alarm on the pulseless form, and see in that imagined spectacle a true representation of the powerlessness of an adulterous world, with all its smiles, blandishments, or threats to move the man who has died to it through sanctification. What are its customs, fashions, follies, pleasures, terrors, or punishments to him? He is dead to them all. There has been a double death. He has been crucified to the world, and the same act of grace has crucified the world unto him. This is the death that is brought in sanctification. Of course there is a new, sweet life that rushes into and fills the soul at the very moment that the death takes place. And O what an unutterably gracious life it is! We cannot speak of it in this chapter, but something of its blessedness will appear in the chapter that follows. We only say that just as when our Saviour died, that instant he lived; so when we, like him, die on the cross, that instant a life, sweet, holy, abundant, and overflowing, thrills and fills us. We let Paul declare what happens: "I am crucified with Christ: nevertheless I live; yet not I, but Christ liveth in me: and the life which I now live in the flesh I live by the faith of the Son of God, who loved me, and gave himself for me."

CHAPTER XXXIV.

IT is the habit of earthly suns to set. It matters not how glorioust he sun and magnificent the rising, the sunset is bound to come. Napoleon, standing on the rocky shore of St. Helena, looking with wistful eyes over the waves toward France, saw the sun of his ambition, that had flashed its burning rays over three continents, set forever in the Atlantic. The strong man stretched out in sickness sees the sun of his physical vigor set forever near the footboard of his bed. Some see their suns go down in Wall Street; others mark it dipping its rim and disappearing in the depths of some loved one's grave.

Even in the regenerated life we have to deplore the fact of setting suns; and if not that, of beclouded and eclipsed suns. What hymns have not been written of shadows, clouds, and night in the spiritual life! Before we realize it a mist comes stealing out of the valley, creeps up the mountain side, and shrouds the light that had begun so promisingly in the first hour of the day. Sometimes "the sun goes down at noon," and we

(282)

have found ourselves groping under stars, where we had only a moment before felt the warm, bright shining of a spiritual noon.

Isaiah speaks of a better experience in the sixtieth chapter and twentieth verse of his book. He presents it in remarkable figurative language: " Thy sun shall no more go down.'' Malachi evidently refers to the same experience when, speaking for God, he says: " Unto you that fear my name shall the Sun of righteousness arise.'' The promise is here made to people that fear God's name; and according to the Bible, which states that the wicked have no fear of God before their eyes, these people were the followers of the Lord. Yet to them is made the promise of this sunrise that should bring healing within and marvelous victory without.

An unsetting sun is something that the soul wants in the spiritual life, and thank God it is just what the Saviour has provided, and is what takes place in sanctification. In the paragraph quoted from Isaiah (lx. 19–22) the following facts regarding the blessing are revealed:

One is that the natural sun and all it betokens is given up. " The sun shall be no more thy light by day.'' In other words, the soul ceases to walk in the light of natural things, or to look for

its happiness in the light of anything that is physical and material and has a sunset in it.   Before
the Unsetting Sun arises we have to bid farewell in
a sense to all other suns and see them go down.
Before the fire of heaven fell on the altar of Abraham the Scripture says "the sun went down."
So let them all go down in the sense of yielding
everything to God in exchange for God.   Sanctification does this for the soul, and so enables us
to look unmoved—yes, rejoicingly—at every sunset that can possibly take place in any realm outside
of the spiritual.

Another feature of this life is that the Lord himself becomes the everlasting light.   The philoso-
phy of the restfulness and blessedness of the sanctified life is at once seen.   God has been made all
and has become all.   He is all; and when a soul
receives him completely, it becomes conscious of
fullness of joy and perfect satisfaction.   God
being full of light—yes, the Light itself—it stands
to reason that the person who has received and
exalted him as the one supreme object of love will
always walk in a spiritual day.   Hence it is that
John from the rocks of Patmos could see the sun
of this world dip itself out of sight in the western
waves of the Mediterranean, and yet feel within
himself that it was still broad day.   And so it is

that the sanctified individual, anywhere and everywhere, can mark the departure of human favor, the flight of fortune, the death of friends, the reverses of time, the loss of health and all else that men count essential to happiness, and realize still within an unbroken peace and content, a steadiness and immovability of heart and life that arises from the fact of an everlasting light from an unsetting sun in the soul, and that sun none other than the Lord himself.

Thus it is that Christians in possession of this blessing have from the depths of dungeon, pain of sick bed, place of uncongenial surrounding, and fire of persecution, rejoiced in spirit instead of complaining and languishing away.

Alienation of friends, misjudgment of motive and life, oppression of power and disappointment of hopes, are all regarded as sunsets by many people. And in the lengthening shadows of these trials they sit down and sigh or weep in the dark and say that all is lost. But sanctification has such a glorious unsetting sun within that the sunsets of this world have failed to effect and change the brightness of the wonderful day it brings.

The writer has seen the street gaslights extinguished in the day, and their light was not missed in the more glorious light of the sun. So the lights of time and this world can be blown out in long lines in the sanctified life, and yet it will be still day in the soul, for within is the unsetting sun. Suppose there were two physical suns in the heavens, one of which dipped out of sight daily in the west: but the other never set, but blazed continually in the sky? Who would be concerned about the disappearance of the first in view of the abiding faithfulness of the second? This is the secret of the serenity of the soul. Let the mountains be carried into the midst of the sea, let every earthly light be blown out, it does not matter. It is high noon in the soul, and God is not only with us, but in us, and we are satisfied.

A third feature connected with the unsetting sun experience is one of spiritual gladness. The twentieth verse says: "The days of thy mourning shall be ended." Thank God there is an experience in the Christian life where sorrow and sighing flee away. That indwelling something which burdens the heart and extorts the unconscious sigh is removed. That something that betrays the Christian into dispositions and actions that occasion heavy sighing afterward is eliminated. And hence the calm mind and peaceful heart indicated by the assertion of ended mourning.

Mourning is not ended in regeneration. Sting-

ing regrets, inability to cast off at once the mortifi-
cation arising from failures, an unaccountable load
upon the heart, sorrowful memories, apprehen-
sions of the future—all these force the sigh to the
lips, and create mourning in the days. Let the
unsetting sun of the sanctified life wheel up in the
sky, and all these mental and spiritual vapors and
chilling shadows flee away. The sun brings healing. Something is done that causes the song and
prayer to rise to the lip as frequently as once formerly complaint and lamentation abounded. The
days of mourning ended means that the days of
rejoicing have begun. The plague of inbred sin
has been removed, the soul has been healed, the
man has learned how to cast every care on Jesus
and to see God in everything, and so very naturally the days of the old time mourning are ended.

It is striking to listen to the testimonies of two
men in an experience meeting, one of whom lives
in a life of sunrises and sunsets, while the other
has over him the unsetting sun. One is ever
speaking of tribulation; the other, of constant victories through the Lord Jesus Christ. One wears
black crape; the other floats a pure white banner.
One seems to have a funeral before his eyes; the
other appears to have been invited to a wedding.

A fourth feature beheld in this remarkable ex-

perience is the recognized godliness of all who
live under the unsetting sun. The paragraph
speaks very plainly here: " Thy people shall be
all righteous." Some suns produce noxious weeds
and nettles, some suns in higher latitudes bring
forth a mixed crop of good and bad plants; but
the unsetting sun looks down upon the flowers and
fruits of righteousness. It possesses the power of
covering the plain, summit, and downward slope
of life at all seasons of the year with the golden
grain of holiness.

Many things are said in derision of the inhabitants who dwell under the unsetting sun. They
are called eccentric, fanatical, and dreamers. But
while that is done, no one disputes their piety; all
agree that they are devout people. There were
those who laughed at Elisha after he got the double
portion of God's spirit; but his life and walk were so
unmistakably heavenly that a woman, seeing him
afar, said to her husband: " I perceive that yonder
is a holy man of God." The disciples after receiving the baptism of the Holy Ghost were said
to be disturbers of the Church and city; but the
very people " took knowledge of them, that they
had been with Jesus." Truly as the sun has a way
of drawing one's likeness on the camera obscura,
so the unsetting sun has the peculiar power of im-

printing the image of Christ upon the soul of that man who lives steadily under its shining.

A fifth feature of the life is seen in the humility that fills the man. The paragraph under examination speaks of a character called "a little one." A curious fact about the unsetting sun is that its shinings produce the little one. It is death to the giants of carnality and self, and causes the individual so to shrink that he soon feels, and is recognized as well, to be one of God's little ones.

The writer has studied the conduct of an unspoiled child, when left to be free and natural. He has observed that he does not court observation, does not thrust himself forward, and is perfectly willing to be overlooked.

God's little one is content to take the lowest seat, unless the call of God or man bids him take a higher position. He knows the luxury of loneliness with Christ and the joy of being set aside and overlooked. The great broad platform, with its rows of chairs for dignitaries of Church and State, is not pined for and sought after. The pompous public introduction and the complimentary valedictory remarks are not craved or sought after by him, but rather like the young prophet at Bethel, he delivers his message, lives his life, and is content to slip away unnoticed and unthanked.

19

How simple are the tastes of God's little one, how few his demands, how patient under disappointment, how unresentful under neglect and wrong. The writer recalls such a minister now in glory, who in visiting his people was filled with pain at the thought of a fowl having been killed for his sake. Another was grossly insulted and cursed on the streets, but like a little child passed humbly on. Still another, while a friend was purchasing goods at the counter of a large fashionable store in one of our great cities, sat down on a low place near his feet in meek unconsciousness of self and surroundings. Great in mind and character, a scholar, writer, and spiritual teacher, there he was with sixty years upon him and greater grace upon him, looking exactly what he was: one of God's little ones.

"Except ye be converted, and become as little children, ye shall not enter into the kingdom of heaven." So spoke the Saviour, and we see the two works of grace in his words. We know of only one grace that makes a person a "little one," and that is the blessing of sanctification.

There are some suns that produce big trees, huge animals, great merchants, and colossal sinners. But we thank God there is another sun whose perpetual shining occasions shrinkage in this world, makes its honors and pleasures appear contemptibly small, takes the puff out of human pride, causes a man to think less and less of himself, turns a giant of sin into a babe in Christ, and actually makes it a joy to be and remain one of God's little ones.

The unsetting sun is wonderful for the production in the life of simplicity, sincerity, unaffected manners, and that complete deliverance from the stiffness, artificiality, and doubleness of life taught and practiced by those who live under a natural sun.

Sanctification does not produce childishness, but childlikeness. The Saviour was a childlike man. The effect of his light shining down on us is to turn the great ones of earth into the little ones of God.

A sixth feature about the unsetting sun is that it produces power. The passage says that "a little one shall become a thousand, and a small one a strong nation." This is certainly wonderful. Some suns cause weakness, other suns awaken strength; but none save the Sun we are writing about can make one man equal to a thousand, and another a strong nation.

As for the last-mentioned fact, a certain queen once dreaded a holy man in her kingdom more

than she did the nation that touched her borders.
The dreaded man seemed to have the resources
and power of a nation in himself.

As for the first fact, we see Finney, who had received the great grace, sweeping over New England and doing the work that a thousand men
had not done. We behold Caughey, after obtaining the baptism of the Holy Ghost in an old
field, accomplishing a work for God in London
that a thousand men had not been able to do.
After Moody received on the streets of New York
the great blessing he had been seeking for weeks,
he became the man of a thousandfold spiritual
strength.

The writer knows of young men now in the
evangelistic work who have been anointed of God
and sent out with their souls on fire with holiness,
who have in a year's time seen more conversions
and sanctifications than is reported by some Annual Conferences. Allowing a board of ten stewards
to each preacher, we see again the thousand men,
and read again with increased thoughtfulness the
words that " a little one shall become or be equal
to a thousand."

But a person must be a " little one " in order to
become one of God's strong ones. When we
think ourselves to be something we become noth-

ing. The way to rise in the spiritual life is to go down. And with humility and loneliness comes the strange force and ability to do great things for God.

Doubtless all of us have seen and known some of these little ones of the kingdom who are equal to a thousand. We have been informed of one in a Southern State who is poor and illiterate, and whose first appearance on his feet in a crowd awakens a feeling of pity in some, and contempt in others, but as he quietly speaks on the power of God descends and people are moved and many are seen wiping away the fast-falling tears.

Miller Willis, of Georgia, was one of these little ones who had power. His simplest word affected people. A salutation from him on the road, his earnest question about the soul's salvation, and his very bearing caused many to think, repent, pray, and to accept Christ.

The author of this book once attended a famous camp meeting. The star preachers and Church celebrities from distant States were there, blazing, coruscating, and exploding like skyrockets harmlessly over the heads of the people for four days. Meanwhile there had not been a tear shed or sigh of penitence heard or a soul at the altar. One afternoon an unknown circuit preacher was put up. As he entered the pulpit the observers could not but be impressed with the meek bearing and holy face of the man. He preached for thirty minutes from the text: " Whatsoever ye do, do all to the glory of God." He did not say a single new or brilliant thing, but he pressed home on heart and conscience the duty of living for God altogether, and for all time. The life urged upon us was one of holiness, and it was pressed by one who was evidently living in it. The effect of that simple sermon by that humble man of God would be hard to describe. A profound conviction, deep humility, weeping tenderness, and desire to prostrate the body before God swept over the audience, and at the first invitation there was a general rush to the altar. Then followed a scene of crying, pleading, agonizing, and shouting the writer will never forget. The preacher had the experience of which this chapter speaks. He lived under the unsetting sun. He was one of God's little ones, and had become equal to a thousand. May God's people everywhere move out of the sunset and twilight and midnight, and from the land of alternating day and night, and settle in the goodly country where the sun never goes down!

CHAPTER XXXV.

THE HOLY WATERS.

THE prophet Ezekiel was granted a number of visions concerning the Church of the future. Among them none is more impressive nor richer in blessed suggestions, and clearer in the description of the coming holiness of the Church than that granted him of the waters bursting out of the holy sanctuary and streaming out over the world. No one can read the first twelve verses of the forty-seventh chapter of the prophecy without realizing the following three facts: One is that a great blessing is to come to the world; another is that the blessing is to come out of the Church. God has been pleased to bless mankind through his people in the past, and will do so to the end. Let every one tempted to Come-out-ism remember that the great approaching grace is to come out of Zion. A third fact taught is that the blessing that is to do much for the race is holiness. The very caption of the chapter reads: " The Vision of the Holy Waters." Moreover, as the waters came out of God's blessed sanctuary, where nothing unclean could enter, how could they be anything else but holy?

Some deeply interesting truths in regard to the holy waters appear in this passage. One is that it starts humbly. It is first seen issuing from under the threshold of the door of the temple. It does not pour down as a cascade beautiful and imposing from the pinnacle of God's house, but is first seen near the floor and ground.

Truly holiness has never originated among the dignitaries and hierarchies, civil or ecclesiastical. Invariably it makes its first appearance among the poor and obscure. When holiness first gushed forth as a distinct blessing for the Church in the New Testament times, it appeared among a band of humble disciples. When it flowed again with marvelous power in the Wesleyan revival, the curious fact of its being confined to the poor was again noticed. It is equally remarkable to-day that the present holiness revival is seen in the Salvation Army, despised by many, and is also sweeping among the humbler members of the various Churches, while the heads and functionaries of the Church, in company with the wealthier classes, look on amazed, disapprovingly, and skeptically at the whole movement. Paul states a solemn truth in the words: "Ye see your calling, brethren, that not many wise men after the flesh, not many mighty, not many noble, are called," while another inspired writer declares that God hath chosen the poor of this world to be rich in faith. The holy water appears under the threshold.

Another fact stated is that the waters came down at the south side of the altar. We are brought at once into the presence and upon the spot itself of sacrifice. Holiness is of God, but cannot flow out to the world except through the sacrifice of the Son of God. The south side of the altar is mentioned. This is the warm, sunny side. There are religious experiences and moralities and ecclesiastical formalities that produce rigidity and coldness. We have known Christian people who, when in their coffins, will scarcely be colder and stiffer than they are now. But holiness touches the south side of our nature, pours sunshine in the soul, and produces the tropical spiritual life. It makes a summer land. Frostiness of manner and chilling speeches are at an end. Fragrance of spirit, melody in the heart, brightness of countenance, and the burning heat of love declares a religious Southland. How the writer wishes that God's people who are cold, if not freezing, on the north side of the altar would come around on the south side and get thawed out and be spiritually warm thereafter for evermore.

19*

The holy waters soon became visible. Who supposes that a fountain gushing up in the church and flowing down the aisles and under the door and out upon the street and down the street could be hidden? If this be the case, who can doubt that when the experience and life of holiness arises in the Church, pours out at the door in the person of the people enjoying it, and streams in every direction toward home, street, and avenue, it will be equally manifest? It could not be concealed on the day of Pentecost, nor in Wesley's time, nor in our time. The strange news is now on every lip, some wondering, some doubting, some believing, but all in the land cognizant of the fact that a peculiar religious experience has arisen in the Church and is sweeping through the land in every direction.

The holy waters could not be stopped; neither can that which it typifies be arrested. The blessed flow of holiness cannot be prevented. A man can divert it from his own heart and life, but he cannot keep it from the world. What folly it would be for one standing down a stream to endeavor to dam it up when it has back of it a fountain, and back of that an inexhaustible subterranean river? Yet what consummate folly is it in one to think that he can arrest the flow of a blessing whose source is in God, and that has a Niagara drop from a world above the stars, and the weight of God's hand and God's will upon it in addition! Did the reader ever try to stop a spring by throwing stones into it, and notice that the water gushed up still, and trickling through the rocks, went on its musical, laughing, triumphant way down the valley? How much less able is one to check that Fountain opened up for sin and uncleanness! And yet there are men foolish enough to try it. It would certainly be a poor fountain if the satire, laughter, and denunciation of a man could dry it up. We notice that in spite of everything in this line it flows on. We have seen what was regarded as a skillful and powerful hand, wielded by a high functionary in the Church, or by one commissioned by that functionary, attempt to seal the fountain and thus stop its flow, when just as they thought the work was done, puff, gush, and lo! the ecclesiastical cement was blown out of sight, and the holy water was gushing again. Think of a man trying to bail the Mississippi River dry with a dipper! Yet have we seen men attempt a far more insane and impossible thing in endeavoring with a dipper of human authority, conferred on them for a few years, to empty the channel of grace of the wonderful stream of holiness flowing out of the very throne and heart of God. With careful hand and calculating eye the dipper is placed in the stream, then suddenly elevated, and its contents flung as far as the authority can throw, when lo! it appears that simply a minnow swimming in the experience has been flung away, while the holy water still flows on.

The water increased. This is taught beautifully. First it reached the ankles, then the knees, then the loins, and finally went over the head. This holds good in the individual case. It is a mistake to think there is no growth or improvement after the blessing of sanctification. Holiness people never say that, but their testimony is that it gets better, deeper, sweeter, every day. And so the time comes when the man is fairly swallowed up in the life, and self is lost to sight.

The figure is true also in a world-wide sense. Many to-day are smiling and sneering at this movement of God. It seems so shallow in its sweep, is confined to such a few camp meetings, has been received by so few of the wealthy and prominent, that no one dreams of being overtaken by it, or its overflowing the land. But the passage teaches that it is an increasing tide, and will steadily rise higher until no one can stand before it. The very pots in the house of the Lord will be holy, the bells on the horses will bear the name, and all will be righteous from the least unto the greatest in those days.

We have only to glance about to see how rapidly the heavenly flood is rising and spreading. In one State alone there are two hundred holiness preachers. Look at the increasing holiness literature, the one hundred holiness periodicals, the sanctified evangelists now covering the country, and the people everywhere who are sweeping into the blessing.

The holy water is to redeem the desert. The writer once saw the Great African Desert. Parched, desolate, and vast as it is, it could be reclaimed by means of the Mediterranean Sea. A greater desert is human life, and greater than man and man's wants is the abundant and never failing grace of God. The vision of the holy waters is but a stream from the sea of the divine fullness. And this ever widening and deepening stream is to redeem and reclaim the spiritual deserts of the world. It seems to have a peculiar bent or tendency in that direction. It moves toward the forsaken and desolate. It rises up to the garrets of a city, descends to the cellars, and goes with its sweet, loving flow to morally abandoned places and lives. Its object is to reclaim the waste and make it bloom like a garden of the Lord.

The holy waters bring life. The remarkable statement made by the prophet is that everything that liveth and moveth shall live where the waters come. Holiness brings life; and, mysterious as it may at first appear, brings it not only to the dead, but to everything that liveth and moveth. It is the regenerated and truly growing Christian who is the first to obtain the blessing.

Here is life added to life. And this is the very experience of this great grace. It is another blessing, containing a deeper and fuller measure of life. Christ spoke of this when he said he came that we might have life, and that we might have it more abundantly. This was what took place at Pentecost; not life, but a more abundant life.

It certainly as a blessing brings life. A man receiving it begins to live indeed in a way worthy of the name. There is life to prayer, to praise, to testimony, to Christian activity, and all this in turn touches and arouses the sinner, and so he obtains life.

The holy waters produce food. They seemed to have the power of making trees spring up of a fruit-bearing character. And this is just what takes place where holiness is received. There spring up under its influence devoted men and women of God, and from them come sermons, testimonies, prayers, songs, and lives that are soul food for the people. Holiness brings food for the soul, rich, strengthening, and satisfying. Millions to-day are perishing for the lack of that food, and are mocked in pulpit and in so-called religious papers by what is termed spiritual provision, that is no more nourishing to the spirit than sawdust to the body.

The holy waters beautified. Look at the picture drawn by the prophet of a river lined with trees. We know of nothing lovelier in nature than the graceful bendings of a river whose flowery shores are lined with lofty and spreading trees. Grassy banks, shadowy nooks and dells, with singing birds, are all concomitant with this scene.

God takes this attractive spectacle in nature to describe the beauty of holiness and the beautifying power of holiness. There is nothing that makes the face and life more attractive and lovely. There comes a beauty of expression, a holy charm in manner evident even to the careless observer. When the Church obtains this grace, she is going to draw and win the world for God.

The holy waters called forth a host of workers.

This thought is suggested by the words, "the fishers shall stand upon it from Engedi even unto En-eglaim." Holiness creates fishermen for souls. This has been and is the invariable result from the day of Pentecost until this day. Let this blessing enter the heart, and workers for God or soul fishermen spring up at once. They want to fish for souls and they know how. Some go out with a line; they seek for and obtain individuals. Others go forth with nets; they have greater gifts or possess more of the Spirit, and so bring in great companies for God. But all are fishermen of souls. The passion for the work is thoroughly aroused. In place after place and church after church the writer has noticed it. When holiness comes to the people of God, they are transformed into burning, tireless workers for him.

They reach from Engedi to En-eglaim. O how we need them from one end of the land to the other; from Boston to San Francisco, from London to Pekin!

A final discovery in regard to holiness, taught by the holy waters, is that it produces a religious experience and life that is unchanging and full of blessedness to others. The remarkable characteristics pertaining to the trees growing by the holy waters brings out this fact.

" Their leaf shall not fade." That is, the religious profession and the corresponding outward appearance of the life are always the same. There are no spells of gloom, fits of dumbness, and bewailings over departed joy and power. The testimony and life are ever bright, strong, and attractive. The leaf, green and fresh, rustles in the wind all the year round.

" The leaf thereof for medicine." Everywhere the experience of holiness shall be told it shall heal some heart, cure doubt, and do good. To speak of what we possess in this beautiful and blessed life is to throw a leaf full of healing on some sin-sick soul. Truly these are some of the leaves that are to bring healing to the nations. Once the writer was relating his experience to a large audience where there was considerable skepticism in regard to the blessing of sanctification. Months afterward he found that the leaf of that open testimony had fallen upon the listening ear of one woman and had brought healing to her soul.

" The fruit thereof shall be for meat." A holy life is moral nourishment. Even people who deny holiness will admit that the lives of godly individuals have stimulated and strengthened them. Truly we feed upon each other, and there is nothing that so nourishes and invigorates the soul as holy teaching and holy living.

"Neither shall the fruit thereof be consumed." This looks like a contradiction to the other statement, but is only one of the paradoxes of the Bible. It means that in the giving forth of the life to others the person himself suffers no waste. As in the miracle of the loaves and fishes, the bread, in spite of constant breaking and distribution, remained unwasted; so this life, in spite of constant demands as well as assaults made upon it, will abide the same. The fruit is not consumed. To the person's delight he finds an unwasting fullness in his experience that lasts not only from day to day and from year to year, but through all the lifetime.

"It shall bring forth new fruit." There will be fresh experiences every day, new works and enterprises for God and man. Men may stone off and pluck away and partake of the fruit of· that life continually, but new fruit, new fruit, new fruit will be seen abounding just as constantly throughout all the days, months, and years of that life.

All this mentioned above takes place, says the prophet, "because their waters they issued out of the sanctuary." Without the waters of holiness, none of these things would or could possibly occur. The vital and unbroken connection with God and the spiritual world is the only explanation of the perennial experience. The constant inflowing of the divine life into our lives will always produce religious activity, moral beauty, unfading freshness of spirit, blessedness to self, and a life abounding in comfort and relief to the spiritually sick, sad, and sinful of the world.

O that the holy waters would begin to flow in every church, appear at the threshold, stream over the land, and fill every heart and the whole world with the knowledge and love and glory and saving power of our God!

THE END.